Heinemann Educational Books Ltd
22 Bedford Square, London WCIB 3HH
P.M.B. 5205, Ibadan · P.O. Box 45314, Nairobi

EDINBURGH MELBOURNE AUCKLAND SINGAPORE
HONG KONG KUALA LUMPUR NEW DELHI
KINGSTON

ISBN 0 435 90171 0

Published under licence by
Heinemann Educational Books (Nigeria) Ltd.,
and printed and bound in Nigeria by
Rosprint Industrial Press Ltd., Ibadan.

Contents

Poems
of
Black Africa

*edited and
introduced by*

Wole Soyinka

HEINEMANN

Poems of Black Africa

This anthology's claim to difference is essentially one of approach. In selecting the poems by theme, my motive is to wean them away from their customary settings of regions, period, style, authorship—natural and valid though of course these are.

The poems embrace most of the experience of the African world—modern and historic—though naturally no claim is made here for an unattainable comprehensiveness of themes; or for their mutual exclusiveness. The overlapping is obvious and frequent. What gives, for instance, the love poems of Dennis Brutus their raw, passionate desperation is the fact that they are just as much poems about love as they are poems of indictment—a word I prefer to "protest"—against the brutish environment from which such emotions are painfully wrenched, that they speak of integral refuge and outer defiance, hope and resolve, within one breath. Even when the poem emerges as essentially tender, its poignancy remains a yet more lacerating accusation.

Senghor's leaping metres of human passion are equally cries of nostalgia for a distant homeland and for that missing essence of himself which he later celebrated more overtly in the doctrine of "negritude". The objects of his love sooner or later become completely identified with homeland; his invocations take on the spiritual urgency of an initiate awaiting fulfilment from ancestral presences.

The nature-saturation of U Tam'si is often inseparable from recognition and assertion of a political self, constantly expanding in its humane concerns. Moods of transcendentalism are infiltrated by political anguish. To quote from "Fragile":

> Endlessly I decalcify my joy
> and lo its hands become islands
> they surpass the Antilles!
> Child I cling no longer to the Zaïre
> I am no more master of my tears
> master of this patchwork of time
>
> what flowers to dress
> for Emmett Till
> child whose soul is bleeding in my own!

One conspicuous quality of U Tam'si's poetry, in company with Rabéarivelo's, Nortje's and others', is that it is structured within a conceptual tradition which embodies essentials of the metaphysics of the African world. Borrowing a word which comes into one of my own recent poems, "animistic", I have tentatively created a special category

for this intense, quasi-mystical poetry. The interfusion of object, thought and spirit is not however peculiar to the African mind. But the quality which separates such poems in this volume from the Surrealists—to take one example—is their avoidance of the Mallarmean extreme, the occidental indulgence which gives an autogenetic existence to the expression of the symbolic-mythical world of the creative imagination, severed arbitrarily from other realities. The poems which are grouped under the heading "Animistic Phases" represent a poetic sensibility which, a little like the English Metaphysicals', creates a "spontaneous landscape of disparities". The Animistic projects not only the material world but also the trivia of incident through cyclic conceptions of death and rebirth, light and darkness, growth and sterility, transience and eternity. Worked through a muscular impact of cumulative images as in much of U Tam'si's poetry, reflective as in Lenrie Peters' "On a wet September morning", or visionary as in Rabéarivelo's "Three Birds", the impulse that weaves the texture of such poems is the basic continuum of thought and matter. If we shed the general meaning attached to the word "superstition", prepare to understand the laws that govern its formulation as belonging to the same laws that enable human beings to imbue incident and matter even with cosmic potential, the animistic perception becomes plain enough.

The remaining categories are straightforward, though, as readily admitted, often arguable. It is perhaps necessary to add that these themes are not preconceived divisions but ones that emerged from the selected poems. A future selection might create new ones or dispense with others.

There is a charge often raised against African poets, that of aping other models, particularly the European. This charge is of course frequently true, even to the extent of outright plagiarism, and covers the entire spectrum of stylistic development: twenty years ago it was quite possible to read poems (of serious intent) which began "Gather ye hibiscus while ye may", while today we are more commonly inundated with the re-creation of Waste Lands of tropical humidity. Dadaisms abound both in their founding innocence and in the revivalist adaptations hallowed by the "beat" generation of America. Even the perverse phase of European decadence has not failed to diffuse its "poisonous ecstasy" through situations clearly shaped in a far different clime, nurtured in the perpetual season of revolution.

All this must be conceded and deplored. But then another question must be asked: whether this has not occurred in all other fields that make up the personalities of new nations. The excesses committed in a small part of the poetic output achieve an importance only for those who fail to see the poet's preoccupations as springing from the same source of creativity which activates the major technological developments: town-planning, sewage-disposal, hydro-electric power. None of these and others—including the making of war—has taken place or will ever again take place without the awareness of foreign thought and culture patterns, and their exploitation. To recommend, on the one hand, that the embattled general or the liberation fighter seek the most sophisticated weaponry from Europe, America or China, while, on the other, that the poet totally expunge from his consciousness all knowledge of a foreign tradition in his own craft, is an absurdity.

A distinct quality in all great poets does exercise a ghostly influence in other writers, but this need not be cause for self-flagellation. The resulting work is judged by its capacity to move ahead or sideways, by the thoroughness of ingestion within a new organic mould, by the original strength of the new entity. Modern African poems which betray traces of an internal dialogue are often accused of alien affectation, but an examination of traditional poetry reveals that it too is built on a densely packed matrix of references (and not, as is sometimes claimed to the contrary, on simplistic narrative). This progression of linked allusions towards an elucidation of the experience of reality is the language of all poets.

History, the contemporary reality and the vision are the purpose of this anthology: the experience of black Africa in the idiom of the poem.

Wole Soyinka

I
Alien Perspective

Belonging

G. Adali-Mortty

You may excel
in knowledge of their tongue,
and universal ties may bind you close to them;
but what they say, and how they feel—
the subtler details of their meaning,
thinking, feeling, reaching—
these are closed to you and me for evermore;
as are, indeed, the interleaves of speech
—our speech—which fall on them
no more than were they dead leaves
in dust-dry harmattan,
although, for years, they've lived
and counted all there is to count
in our midst!

The Right Road

David Diop

Brothers whose youth they would tear to shreds
Do not look for the truth among their simpering words
Among paternalist yes-men and backstairs betrayals
Do not look for beauty in that restless mask
Soaking in perfume their hideous sores
Nor for love in those exposed thighs
Coining adventure in pick-up bars
Truth Beauty Love
Is the workman smashing the deadly composure of their drawing-
    room
  the woman who walks by, sensuous and solemn
  he kiss that crosses the frontiers of calculation
and the flowers between couples and the child in the arms it loves
is everything they have lost brothers
And what together we will unroll down the roads of the world

Europe

Mazisi Kunene

Europe, your foundations
Are laid on a rough stone.
Your heart is like cobwebs
That are dry in the desert.

Your children fill us with fear:
They are like the young of a puff adder
Who devour the flesh of their parent.

Once I believed the tales.
Once I believed you had breasts
Over-flowing with milk.

I saw you rushing with books
From which the oracles derive their prophecies.
I heard you in the forest
Crying like wolves,
Breaking the bones of your clans.

I know the hardness of your visions:
You closed the doors
And chose the bridegroom of steel.

You chose her not to love
But because she alone remained
Dedicated to silence.

From her you made your prophecies
And summoned the oracles:
You laughed at the blind men
But you yourself were blind,
Struggling in this great night.

Children have inherited the fire.
They blow its flames to the skies
Burning others in their sleep.

What will the sun say?
The sun will laugh
Because it burnt out cradles from age to age.

To Susan Sontag, with love   *Taban Lo Liyong*

Part I
in mans greatest intellectual age sometimes called mythopoeic
he gave rivers tongues trees ears sky eyes mother earth oozed
    with life
words were very gods
why but to make witnesses
all witnesses police judges erinyes

we remained human while that age lasted and its shadow
    covered us

but enlightenment encroached this sensitive terrain
drove imagination behind saying we rational creatures be
and down with superstition
man shall live by reason alone
as if this was first time human intellect had beheld these views
enlightenment prophesied god dead
snuffing out divine in us
sacredness was dead for good
we caught unsuperstition like flu

mans feedback is fear
and superstition his homeostasis
and religion his lifebelt
at end of his tether man lives by myths and dies by daring
    ignorance

ancient greeks in modesty moulded earth and gave objects so
    made supernames
correlatives of force and power in man
heartsearchingly deeming it better man surrendered potency to
    objects

and nouns abstract
making himself harmlesser towards strangers and neighbours
and a serf to his own metacreatures
whose feats feast games
he observed with awe from distance
dared not imitate challenge

scapegods man made
and placed on olympuses
had megahuman exploits men enjoyed in telling only
and bore blames for his immodesty
and glowed with pride in his success
always picking tabs and paying insurance
to experience lodged in subconscious
for acts omitted or committed

with lights we came on scene in time machines
and thought first generator toy
and dismantled wheel rod indicators
shaking cosmology out of balance

human injunctions aimed and austere
had gone forth to fear gods
and not prod them
and respects to locks of nestors
and noncontradiction of continuity with observation of line
    in middle
mans mind cant carry much
nor follow road straight
but if remains on earth will stay safe
intuition is not practical
greeks flew by proxy
divines kept dark ages bright
inquisition lost last battle against madness
without fear without superstition nails are painted red
and fermi munches japanese
a villain after galileo
at least newton repented

firmer wax sends daedalus hit very sun
and goddic mysteries flouted without fear
everyman own god

puny nietzsches strut
bloated frogs
race of supermen has come
but where superhumanists
with guilt gone
was auschwitz far
sacredness is dead
and biroshima invented
without superstition
denigrated godtheidea
to confront mantheideamaker
more nearly

our death machines be twostage rocket
launched on humanists laps
by scientists
they killed witches and sought for stone
keeping idea alive
we are enlightened now and burnt by fire overexposure
the wring hands
chorus bastard humanists
rebels against ignorance set acknowledging us
drilling efficiency in thick skulls and making us robots
god knows what else our fates
from abundant imagination lodged in impractical timid
     humanists

scientists put to work magic
poets planned and blueprinted in classrooms
lurid attics and pulpits
and politicians would outdo alexanderandcaesar
as taught in school
everybodys tomb a pyramid and shrine
we teach iliad for war
right and wrong troy is ours

damn guy fawkes for gunpowder
but printing machine crushed noble castles
far and near amen

aeiou rimbaud sought your pregnant secrets
as if grammarians hadnt stuffed us full
with correct usage agreements
miss verb and mister person
and lord bacon urged exactness
unto him machines
shakespeare
life blows like wind
of no signification
what its worth
and world a stage
for how many roles
of angelsanddevils

sartres waiter dribbles precarious tray
full of eats and drinks and poisons
accomplished actor iago
jean uncommon actor
manipulating words
ergo cinc
manipulating cultivated physiques
veritable foyers

goethes alter ego mephistopheles
rewarded belle in saigon
drops napalm and bomb
wildes science for sciences sake
is come
rejoice
capacity for variety sensations is dostoyevskys work on paper
pavlovs moved from dogs to flesh and mind
overacute consciousness is disease with own fundamental laws
common to intellects elect
screws them tight

and forces moment to own conclusion
no matter the end
fyodor gets pleasure killing story
scientist discovering law
lover consummates sex orgasm
murderer kills victim

everything permitted
existentists technicians prepare biological warfare
aristotles literary sublime is literature
imitation
so metaliterature cybernetics

inhuman use
suffering
oedipus cleanses us incest
and murder
and bloodier macbeth
washes cleaner pogroms
and roastedpeasants best detergents

granddad noah dead drunk near mississippi
triple summer murders
and sharpeville bloodbath
divine comedy be bloodier
for sake of dantes enemies
burn in hell
and ours hereandthere eliot
we loster generation
with war objective correlative of might and something else

ive never heard bomb
but beethoven shot and tschaikovsky answered
guernica mangled few
picasso criminally dismembered all
and unborn gorgons head
moore made models for pills copy
and japanese bomb mass produce

general piet mondrian directs bombing operations
complete maps enemy territory
squared paddies green jungles ports rivers bridges deltas roads
    rails
ready bombing
marines today tomorrow when escalation authorized

homer wins pulitzer prizes
outstanding warreporting
those deranged war cured sanatoria
but brainmixed by joice
teach universities

technocrats
beautiful hirelings
magnates
single
corporate
governing servants
Efficiency Almighty
computers in hand
massmedia in mouth
aesthetics for minds
missiles as comets
go worshipping unconcerned
about myliverandourhobbyhorse
guinea pigs die our first breaths
we less equal than other pigs
strong carlyle orders workanddoubtnot
and robots drive through green and yellow
till all is red

books on sex banned
but more potent tripped
milton honoured
but mute betters forgot

forget innocents and sadists
but preserve masochists for private consumption
publicly honour heroes
distinguished murderers

temperance societies filled donations
teetotallers get grand ovations
but not alcohol only intoxicate
KNOWLEDGE does
homer turned keats on
elgin marbles broke his heart
poor sweet nightingale

psychedelics may be harmful your health
but surrealism destroys than pills
adverse effects literary materials
on human bodyandmind
be investigated by houseunamericanactivities
sick in utopias criminal
should be criminal in ours
to be bright
and all intellectuals be rounded up
on ground intoxication
with ideas
and disturbance of natural mediocrity of man
we shall revive
the grand ancient society
for preservation of Ignorance

man
thoroughly dull creature since civilizations came and went
centuries piled top centuries
to make man less ignorant
after that
she has to spend most her life and energy being reminded
of bits of what should know to make death kit

ps
between the committed man
moral and blaming
and manofscience
there is only a difference of impracticality
the timid gropes for standardization and equality
the tradesman delivers on a platter the finished order
mixed with blood
and limbs
and horror
and overefficiency
amen.

Heart of the Matter

Ifeanyi Menkiti

It is the vital deprivation
Of the underdeveloped countries
That they do not have factories
For the manufacture of chewing gum
Nor grandstands for Coca-Cola dispensation.

London Impressions

Arthur Nortje

I

Out of the Whitehall shadows I pass
into a blaze of sun as sudden as fountains.
Between the bronze paws of a lion
a beatnik stretches his slack indifferent muscles.

Nelson's patina of pigeon shit
hardly oppresses that plucky sailor. Cloudbanks
lazily roll in the blue heavens beyond.
The birds home in on seas of seed.

Foil tins float on the dusty water.
The walls are full of faces and thighs.

I smoke a Gold Leaf close to the filter,
viewing dimly the circles of traffic.

The isle is full of Foreign Noises
that jangle in trafalgar square,
England expects every tourist
to do his duty now the Pound is sickly.

II

A girl plays games with mirrors
in Hyde Park while I'm half-suggestive
with the dolly scanning a volume idly.
In the flare of an instant it takes to light
a cigarette:
against her treetrunk comes to lean
the ugliest bloke that you have ever seen.
Predictably they disappear
through the distance of August green.

The nymph on the grass behind
proves her point by blinding my return look.
She picks her black bag up and drifts on further,
not helpful as to whether I should follow.
Meanwhile a huge Alsatian sniffs my loose boots,
the gentleman with the leash exchanges gossip.

Sun, you are all I have:
the grass already welcomes the brown leaves.
I do not want to cross the road again,
having learnt the value of other faces,
acquired the pace and tone of other voices.

And big red buses; I thought I would never catch
sight of the gentle monsters
When I was young and shackled for my sharpness
in the Union of South Africa.

999 Smiles   Atukwei Okai
To Guy Warren

Nine hudnred and ninety -nine smiles
Plus
One quarrle ago, our eyes and our
Hearts
Were in agreement full that still

The sun rises in the East
And sets int he West that
Still
Rains fall from above
Downward to the earth
That
Still smoke rise from the
Earth , reaching for the sky
That
Still our earth is round and
Not flat like a spread-out
Mat

And yet ..
          See where
                    Today
You have
          Gone
                    To sit......
Throwing ......
                    Stones
                              At us ....
Poisonous ...
                    Stones ...
                              At us...
Satanic ....
                    Stones......
                              At us..............

And if I still had my hands
On my shoulders I should raise
One of my hands above my
Head
And gauge and catch your
Stones, one by one, while they
Were still hot in the cool
Air,

and yet . . .
       see where . . .
                  today

you have
       gone
          to sit . . .
hurling . . .
       stones . . .
            at us . . .

hurling . . .
       stones . . .
            at us . . .

infernal . . .
       stones . . .
            at us . . .

sinister . . .
       stones . . .
            at us . . .

But all the same, I shall not even
Utter your name, lest the fast and
Faithful
Winds repeat it to the hearing of
Our ancestors who are asleep
With
Their eyes, but not asleep with
Their ears, lest our ancestors

Angrily
Rise out of their nest and
Breathe out the winds that can
Shake
Till it breaks, the decayed drooping
Branch
upon which
            of all
                    people
you today
        have gone
                to sit ...
hurling ...
            stones ...
                    at us ...
wrathful ...
            stones ...
                    at us ...
saddening ...
            stones ...
                    at us ...

Charging precisely to our
Head, and if I still had my
Hands about me, I would
Gather
Your stones into a heap, and
Leave them there to lie till
Some morrow when we might
Use

Them to bring down to the warm
Tongues of some fire, fleshy
Birds, that above our heads are
Perched,

I had my hands with me, I would
Catch
And keep your stone without thinking
Of throwing them back at you—but
The hands too soon you have stolen away
With
you
   to where
       today
you have
     gone
       to perch
throwing . . .
       stones . . .
            at us . . .
venomous . . .
       stones . . .
            at us . . .
spiteful . . .
       stones . . .
            at us . . .

nine hundred and ninety-nine smiles
plus
one quarrel ago our eyes and our
hearts
were in agreement full that still

When a man lifts his foot, it is
Forward
That he places it, that still, each
Human
Being owns only ten fingers on two
Hands

II
Ancestors and Gods

a squirrel crosses my way
while on a trip
then luck is mine
but when it's a cheetah
or wild cat that crosses there
I turn and go back.

I knock my right foot on stone
while on a trip
I melt in joy
since I shall be overfed
but when it's the left
I turn and go back.

I slip in my shirt
the inside coming out
I jump in merriment
for I shall be overfed.

the first being
I meet in the feeble dawn
is an old woman
I turn to my blanket
it's all ill luck.

I dream my relative dead
in midst of sweet slumbers
I wake in joy
knowing he's overfed
the previous night
and if I dream I am dead
I rejoice
for growing an inch.
and if I dream
of my ideal girl
then I lose hope
the answer is no.

38

I wake up in the morning
and find my teeth shaking
and loose
surely I know
they went eating excreta
while soul courted in fairyland.

A hen crows
it must be killed
bad omen
a dog howls
instead of barking
the village owner
is at death's door
and if I walk on my head
then I am dead.

She Has Not Dreamt   *Jared Angira*

*According to Luo tradition, when a man dies, his widow cannot be married
to another man until the widow admits verbally that she has had sexual
intercourse with her deceased husband through a dream*

She has not dreamt
my father
and none can
to wedlock mat guide her,
the papyrus mat
whistles silence
the cold drives the dagger
across her breast
and the archaeologists
wrestle her bones . . .

I enter the pier
where lie some wrecks
of ships of the past

uncoated, nude, lone
teeth protrude
like carcasses
the vultures left
when they left in a hurry.
Pebbles of broken pots
after regeneration
wrap to knees
what I excavate.

An overseer,
contrast to science
whips my bony back—
I drowse, faint and rise
to the lash . . .
SHE DENIES EVER
DREAMING MY FATHER.

She wears his clothes
In the mergence of rays
a siren howls
for me to storm
the sea of solitude
a boulder roll from the top
of Mount of Life
knocks my ankle
. . . the venereal that eats
my salad potency
a wind whispers goodbye
to the Three Stones
around my being
a father in my chapel
four times pardons his chest
Hail Mary, Queen of Grace.

In escaping
crusts of salt
fall on my ankle wound

the cause of my suicide
the twain ... the twain
what of the orbits
of those scattered stars
and satellite moons?
She stands aloof
AND DENIES
EVER DREAMING MY FATHER.

Conjugation banned
by established authority
... no more lollipop
on population expansion
and the howdah is nationalized
(or traditionalized?)
her stalactite heart is in pain
from a septic ulcer

She stands on laru
a green stanchion.
I question the turn
'Oppidans unwanted'
Never been to town
still 'Oppidans unwanted'
and she insists of never
KNOWING MY FATHER.

Walking across the limbo
the very grave
where in silent quietness we laid him
I fail to identify
believable?
All graves look alike
with frowning daisies,
My mother, closes her mouth
and laughs at me
the cave of her mouth
is dark and rusty

for the treasure therein
it is a CLOSED AREA:
I enter
The
The Faculty of Ferments.

Songs of Sorrow

Kofi Awoonor

Dzogbese Lisa has treated me thus
It has led me among the sharps of the forest
Returning is not possible
And going forward is a great difficulty
The affairs of this world are like the chameleon faeces
Into which I have stepped
When I clean it cannot go.*

I am on the world's extreme corner,
I am not sitting in the row with the eminent
But those who are lucky
Sit in the middle and forget
I am on the world's extreme corner
I can only go beyond and forget.

My people, I have been somewhere
If I turn here, the rain beats me
If I turn there the sun burns me
The firewood of this world
Is for only those who can take heart
That is why not all can gather it.
The world is not good for anybody
But you are so happy with your fate;
Alas! the travellers are back
All covered with debt.

Something has happened to me
The things so great that I cannot weep;

* Colloquial: it (the faeces) will not go (come off)

I have no sons to fire the gun when I die
And no daughters to wail when I close my mouth
I have wandered on the wilderness
The great wilderness men call life
The rain has beaten me,
And the sharp stumps cut as keen as knives
I shall go beyond and rest.
I have no kin and no brother,
Death has made war upon our house;

And Kpeti's great household is no more,
On'y the broken fence stands;
And those who dared not look in his face
Have come out as men.
How well their pride is with them.
Let those gone before take note
They have treated their offspring badly.
What is the wailing for?
Somebody is dead. Agosu himself
Alas! a snake has bitten me
My right arm is broken,
And the tree on which I lean is fallen.

Agosi if you go tell them,
Tell Nyidevu, Kpeti, and Kove
That they have done us evil;
Tell them their house is falling
And the trees in the fence
Have been eaten by termites;
That the martels curse them.
Ask them why they idle there
While we suffer, and eat sand.
And the crow and the vulture
Hover always above our broken fences
And strangers walk over our portion.

Ancestral Faces   *Kwesi Brew*

They sneaked into the limbo of time,
But could not muffle the gay jingling
Brass bells on the frothy necks
Of the sacrificial sheep that limped and nodded after them;
They could not hide the moss on the bald pate
Of their reverent heads;
And the gnarled barks of the wawa tree;
Nor the rust on the ancient state-swords;
Nor the skulls studded with grinning cowries;
They could not silence the drums,
The fibre of their souls and ours—
The drums that whisper to us behind black sinewy hands.
They gazed
And sweeping like white locusts through the forests
Saw the same men, slightly wizened,
Shuffle their sandalled feet to the same rhythms,
They heard the same words of wisdom uttered
Between puffs of pale blue smoke:
They saw us,
And said: They have not changed!

Olokun   *J. P. Clark*

I love to pass my fingers
(As tide thro' weeds of the sea
And wind the tall fern-fronds)
Thro' the strands of your hair
Dark as night that screens the naked moon!

I am jealous and passionate
Like Jehovah, God of the Jews,
And I would that you realize
No greater love had woman
From man than the one I have for you!

But what wakeful eyes of man,
Made of the mud of this earth,
Can stare at the touch of sleep
The sable vehicle of dream
Which indeed is the look of your eyes?

So drunken, like ancient walls
We crumble in heaps at your feet;
And as the good maid of the sea,
Full of rich bounties for men,
You lift us all beggars to your breast.

Breath   *Birago Diop*

Listen more to things
Than to words that are said.
The water's voice sings
And the flame cries
And the wind that brings
The woods to sighs
Is the breathing of the dead.

Those who are dead have never gone away.
They are in the shadows darkening around,
They are in the shadows fading into day,
The dead are not under the ground.
They are in the trees that quiver,
They are in the woods that weep,
They are in the waters of the rivers,
They are in the waters that sleep.
They are in the crowds, they are in the homestead.
The dead are never dead.

Listen more to things
Than to words that are said.
The water's voice sings
And the flame cries

And the wind that brings
The woods to sighs
Is the breathing of the dead.
Who have not gone away
Who are not under the ground
Who are never dead.

Those who are dead have never gone away.
They are at the breast of the wife.
They are in the child's cry of dismay
And the firebrand bursting into life.
The dead are not under the ground.
They are in the fire that burns low
They are in the grass with tears to shed,
In the rock where whining winds blow
They are in the forest, they are in the homestead.
The dead are never dead.

Listen more to things
Than to words that are said.
The water's voice sings
And the flame cries
And the wind that brings
The woods to sighs
Is the breathing of the dead.

And repeats each day
The Covenant where it is said
That our fate is bound to the law,
And the fate of the dead who are not dead
To the spirits of breath who are stronger than they.
We are bound to Life by this harsh law
And by this Covenant we are bound
To the deeds of the breathings that die
Along the bed and the banks of the river,
To the deeds of the breaths that quiver
In the rock that whines and the grasses that cry

To the deeds of the breathings that lie
In the shadow that lightens and grows deep
In the tree that shudders, in the woods that weep,
In the waters that flow and the waters that sleep,
To the spirits of breath which are stronger than they
That have taken the breath of the deathless dead
Of the dead who have never gone away
Of the dead who are not now under the ground.

Listen more to things
Than to words that are said.
The water's voice sings
And the flame cries
And the wind that brings
The woods to sighs
Is the breathing of the dead.

Vanity

Birago Diop

If we tell, gently, gently
All that we shall one day have to tell,
Who then will hear our voices without laughter,
Sad complaining voices of beggars
Who indeed will hear them without laughter?

If we cry roughly of our torments
Ever increasing from the start of things,
What eyes will watch our large mouths
Shaped by the laughter of big children
What eyes will watch our large mouths?

What heart will listen to our clamouring?
What ear to our pitiful anger
Which grows in us like a tumour
In the black depth of our plaintive throats?

When our Dead come with their Dead
When they have spoken to us with their clumsy voices;
Just as our ears were deaf

To their cries, to their wild appeals
Just as our ears were deaf
They have left on the earth their cries,
In the air, on the water where they have traced their signs
For us, blind deaf and unworthy Sons
Who see nothing of what they have made
In the air, on the water , where they have traced their
signs.

And since we did not understand our dead
Since we have never listened to their cries
If we weep, gently, gently
What heart will listen to our clamouring,
What ear to our sobbing hearts?

The Bond   *Mazisi Kunene*

Gumede son of Bdaba, here I am .
I have come to present
This grinding stone of Masilela, my mother.
It is heavy, as though she weighted it with magic.
She left on it the gourd of her heart.
Do not forget it at Mpembeni house
Lest the vermin multiply on it .
Life may put a curse on us
Since we did not behave like her children.
If he be present who has a thousand ribe
Do not allow him to deceive you,
Promising place for it on the fertile lands.
Hold it sacred knowing in it is our soul

Cycle

Mazisi Kunene

Part I

So many are asleep under the ground,
When we dance at the festival
Embracing the earth with our feet.
Maybe the place on which we stand
Is where they also stood with their dreams.
They dreamed until they were tired
And handed us the tail with which we shall dance.
Even the weeds emerge in their praise.
Yesterday there were vast villages
We too shall follow their path,
Our dust shall arise at the gathering place
And the child will dance alone on our grounds.

Part II

How many generations
We dance over
When we are happy at the feast.
They scream from the outskirts,
Where we shall not reach with our feet.
Our eyes break into the sea of the night
When we arrive at the disputed field
Where people fight for a resting place,
Competing with the generations of antiquity.
Their tried voices rise
Rising with their songs
That will remain after the festival.

To the Living

Richard Ntiru

Only those
Who have survived
The final anaesthetization;
Those who have enacted the final epilogue;
Only those

Have the prescient perception
Of the inner idea of life
And can partake of the spectral dance;

Only they
Have the inner knowledge
Of the numbing nutation
On gravestill nights when nude priests,
In mortal ecstasy,
Bless multicoloured antiamulets
On virgin pelvicbone amphorae
And celebrate prenatal deathdays
To the rhythm of the drum of death
Struck with the thighbone
Of him who died on his bridal night.

These are they
Who have bartered their bones
And submitted to the savage salvation
Of the caustic dew of the cold grave;
Only these
Understand the eloquence of the silence
Between two echoes in a haunted cave.

Who but they
Who walk beyond the twilight glimmer
Between sleep and waking,
Who bask in nocturnal sunlight
And breathe the cool diurnal darkbreeze,
Who have experienced
The realization of the inevitable dream,
Know the revitalizing power of the stilled blood?

But we,
We who clutch at tattered totems
And turn away from solar solace
When the innocence butter
Melts in our hands at the ordeal,

We who raise open hands in supplication to Nyabingi—
Hands that would embrace—
What dream are we capable of?

The Prophecy *Richard Ntiru*

Who shall console the veiled woman
who buries her head in her wet hands,
who weeps at the folly of weeping
tears that won't dissolve the sour truth
that in a deal between God and man,
God always takes the better bargain?

The cause is as big as a grain of millet.

Who shall console the lonely woman
who sits in a kraal, on this lonely mound,
who sits and sobs,
each sob a knife thrust in her heavy heart,
each tear a drop of blood from her bleeding heart,
each sigh a bubble of life bursting from her lungs?

The cause is as big as a grain of millet.

Who shall feel the sad music
that rides on the waves of her sobs and tears
and rocks her hunched-up form
as she clenches her quivering jaws
gnawing at the eternally elusive truth
that who has known no enemy in his life
idolizes the body?

Who shall share her singular experience
that the cause as as big as a grain of millet?

Why should she sing
when the cause is no more?

Why should she mourn the loss
of what she got beyond expectation?
Why should she resent the equivocal tongue
of the Three Sisters at whose shrine the Oracle said:

> "Daughter of Misfortune
> A woman is never barren
> In your last egg, I see a daughter
> But beware of the bull's horn."

Whose cloudy eye will look back with her,
rocking her baby as she rocks her grief now,
singing to her mirror with maternal glee:

> never go into the sun
> lest you melt away
> never sit in the cold
> lest your blood congeal
> never walk in the dawn
> lest the dew erode your feet
> never walk too far
> lest you stumble and fall
> never come in the bull's way
> lest the prophecy come true

Who shall share her singular experience
that the cause is as big as a grain of millet?

Who shall hear the hunters' cry,
like leaves singing on the wings of the wind,
the hunting dogs' barks of conquest
like the tribal drums after the war victory;
who shall hear the hunter's cry
that drew the daughter to the gate,
her agemates' ululation
that lured the daughter to the kraal,
the women's circular spinning gyration
that raised the daughter to this lonely mound,
the hunter's spears shimmering with victory
that dazzled the daughter's eyes

and overturned her balance,
thrusting her on the fatal point of the bull's horn
negligently sticking out in the kraal?

Who shall hear the hunter's cry
that brought the prophecy home?

Who shall sit beside this lonely veiled woman
to give a consoling answer to her sodden question:
"Who can prevent the liver of ill luck
from breaking the knife?"

Benin Woman
Odia Ofeimun

Under the smouldering sun oi
this angry afternoon
you sum up the ancient city
in a quaint, moonlit stare, indifference.

Rooted to the earth
left alone to sing in bronze
your sad story

You become for me, the symbol
of my snuffed-out love,
(cheap mushroom for a famished night's palate)
a totem of innocent death

The speech of your eurythma transforms
my erstwhile derision to worship;
And I suddenly realize
you put a stopped on your road
to oil the rusted joints of
bittered emotions

Emotan, I make my solemn prostration
to your guts!—your footpath

strewn with broken pots, shattered clay
trod on by the heavy, rough-hewn feet
of your day.

And how I wish some woman now
would bear your name anew, for my sake
But your sky inspires awe
with its exaggeration of mutating stars.
your sky is red, all red;
red, red clouds affirm your loneliness
which today you confound me with

I dance to your song of bronze.

(*from* Idanre)   *Wole Soyinka*

IV   The Beginning

Low beneath rockshields, home of the Iron One
The sun had built a fire within
Earth's heartstone. Flames in fever fits
Ran in rock fissures, and hill surfaces
Were all aglow with earth's transparency

  Orisa-nla, Orunmila, Esu, Ifa were all assemble
  Defeated in the quest to fraternize with man

Wordlessly he rose, sought knowledge in the hills
Ogun the lone one saw it all, the secret
Veins of matter, and the circling lodes
Sango's spent thunderbolt served him a hammer-head
His fingers touched earth-core, and it yielded

  To think, a mere plague of finite chaos
  Stood between the gods and man

54

He made a mesh of elements, from stone
Of fire in earthfruit, the womb of energies
He made an anvil of paks and kneaded
Red clay for his mould. In his hand the Weapon
Gleamed, born of the primal mechanic

      And this pledge he gave the heavens
      I will clear a path to man

His task was ended, he declined the crown
Of deities, sought retreat in heights. But Ire
Laid skilled siege to divine withdrawal. Also
For diplomatic arts, the Elders of Ire prevailed;
He descended, and they crowned him king.

      Who speaks to me in chance recesses
      Who guides the finger's eye

Now he climbs in reparation, who anointed
God head in carnage, O let heaven loose the bol
of last season's dam for him to lave his fingers
Merely, and in the heady line of blood
Vultures down: Merely.

And in the lungstreams of depleted pastures
Earth is flattened. O the Children of Ogun
Reaped red earth that harvest, rain
Is chidlren's reeds and the sky a bird-pond
Unitl my god has bathed his hands

      Who brings a god to supper, guard him well
      And set his place with a long bamboo pole

Ogun is the lasoivious god who takes
Seven gourdiets to war. One for gunpowder,
One for charms, two for palm wine and three
Air- sealed in polished bronze make
Storage for his sperms

My god Ogun, orphans' Shield, his home
Is terraced hills self-surmounting to the skies
Ogun path-maker, he who goes fore where other gods
Have turned. Shield of orphans, was your shield
In-spiked that day on sheltering lives?

Yet had he fled when his primal task was done
Fugitive from man and god, ever seeking hills
And rock bounds. Idanre's granite offered peace
And there he dwelt until the emissaries came—
Lead us king, and warlord.

> Who speaks to me I cannot tell
> Who guides the hammer's flight

Gods drowse in boredom, and their pity
Is easy roused with lush obsequious rites
Because the rodent nibbled somewhat at his yam,
The farmer hired a hunter, filled him with wine
And thrust a firebrand in his hand

> We do not burn the woods to trap
> A squirrel; we do not ask the mountain's
> Aid, to crack a walnut.

Traditional (from the Yoruba)

Now I will chant a salute to my Ogun
O Belligerent One, you are not cruel.
The Ejemu, foremost chief of Iwonran Town,
He who smartly accoutres himself and goes to the fight.
A butterfly chances upon a civet-cat's excrement and flies high
    up into the air.
Ogun, don't fight against me.
Don't play with me.

Just be to me a giver of good luck.

You said you were playing with a child.

I saw much blood flowing from the girl's private parts.

Ogun, don't fight against me.

Don't play with me.

You said you were playing with a boy.

I saw much blood flowing from the boy's private parts.

Ogun, don't fight against me.

Don't play with me.

You were playing with a pigeon.

The pigeon's head was torn from its neck.

Ogun, don't fight against me.

Don't play with me.

You were playing with a sheep.

The sheep was slaughtered with a knife.

Ogun, don't fight against me.

Don't play with me.

You were playing with a male dog.

The male dog was beheaded.

Ogun, don't fight against me.

Don't play with me.

O Belligerent One, you are not cruel.

The Ejemu, foremost chief of Iwonran Town,

He who smartly accoutres himself and goes to the fight.

A butterfly chances upon a civet-cat's excrement and flies high
     up into the air.

There were initially sixteen chiefs.

In the town called Ilagbede, of these the paramount chief was
          Ejitola,

Ejitola Ireni, son of Ogun,

The blacksmith who, as he speaks, lightly strikes his hammer
     upon his anvil repeatedly.

Son of He who smashes up an iron implement and forges it
     afresh into new form.

Son of He who dances, as if to the emele drum music, while
holding the hollow bamboo poles used for blowing air upon the
coal embers fire in his smithy. He who swells out like a toad
as he operates the smithy's bellows.

I will chant a salute to my Ogun.

O Belligerent One, you are gentle, the Ejemu, foremost chief of
Iwonran, He who smartly accoutres himself and goes to the fight.

Some people said Ogun was a failure as a hunter.

Ogun therefore killed a man and packed the corpse into a
    domestic fire.

Then he killed the man's wife and packed her corpse behind
    the fireplace.

When some people still said that Ogun was a failure as a
    hunter,

The sword which Ogun was holding in his hand,

He stuck into the ground on a river bank.

The sword became a plant, the plant now called "labelabe".

Hence the saying "No ceremony in honour of Ogun can be
    performed at the river-side,

Without Labelabe's getting to know of it".

It is I, a son of Akinwamde, who am performing.

I do good turns for people of decent appearance.

The Fulani Creation Story   *Traditional (from the Fulani)*

At the beginning there was a huge drop of milk.

Then Doondari came and he created the stone.

Then the stone created iron;

And iron created fire;

And fire created water;

And water created air.

Then Doondari descended the second time.

And he took the five elements

And he shaped them into man.

But man was proud.

Then Doondari created blindness, and blindness defeated man.

But when blindness became too proud,

Doondari created sleep, and sleep defeated blindness;

But when sleep became too proud,

Doondari created worry, and worry defeated sleep;

But when worry became too proud,
Doondari created death, and death defeated worry.
But then death became too proud,
Doondari descended for the third time,
And he came as Gueno, the eternal one.
And Gueno defeated death.

II On the Edge

Okogbule Wonodi

I wait on the shore
for the turning tide
and for seabirds, mouthful,
with shrimps caught on wet marshes.

Around me the sands burn,
films of heat rise
from under my feet
and mud walls crack;
yet there's a cackle in public houses.

For I, that farm at noon,
eat of other farmers
and seek to fish at the day's end . . .

But I have had to wait,
patiently,
waited for the return of Aka
who, untouched by the flood
at the flux of day and night,
baits his sire's hooks
and looks years and years hence.

I'll wait for his return,
wait for the turning tide
as tree trunks grow
out of the silts of past floods.

III
Animistic Phases

Hitch-Hike
Jared Angira

The Memory
stands like a cracked bronze statue
in a museum
talking, smiling when we are tired with life

we struggle to frustrate
old pressures on our backs,
rain beats the ground, we flounder, slip

having travelled far, I came upon
mountains of histories,
dead lakes on which libraries are erected
wheels of the train
passed us
chattering like idiots
billows of future meandered, followed the rainbow

sugar and salt are same to a dying tongue
I must try to join
the broken particles of my slate
though the line will be there
and only keen eyes will see
that my slate broke once, and on waking was joined—
the slate with a line, not black, not white
I'll hitch-hike with pilgrims to Vietnam, the boss has said.

A Look in the Past
Jared Angira

Once I was a lizard
cheeky and harmless
and built clouds
that the heat
never could melt

I learnt
of the transanimation
into a monitor
deaf to all spikes
a dweller of two worlds . . .

ere my breath had settled
my back grew rough—
my teeth went chisel-like
. . . a crocodile
lurking in sandy seafloor

then one day I died
but knocked my head
on the sharp gravestone
that woke me up
to find me winged
tough-clawed and a scavenger . . .
I was an eagle.

I went on sojourn
and my red eyes blue'd
till I turned priestly—
pigeoned
till we came to Guernica
where they pinched my olive branch
and gave me a bone

when next I stopped
I was gliding
mutilated . . .
the mongoose pursued me in hideways

I shall go back
to the formless clouds
and melt myself into rain
then shall I land in the plantation
and mate with the secondary roots
of the old fig tree.

Stream, Beach and Shadow: Scene

heavy, like snails, the pebbles seem to move
with a stone paleness of pain
downstream, reluctant towards the law
of gravity, the
                    bank under my buttocks
is root-firm, earth's earth, and unlike

green yeast of moss in shy
patches germinating to attention
when the sky is allover blue simply
and soft, I think

With the moon gone that was
at dawn a crescent of ash
I flick sunlight off my toes
                    and rise
among willow fragrances, leaves,
and the fellow-travelling shadow:
                                        mute
little prisoner, the soul apologizes, how
you diminish or do you
                        fear separation? hearing

the gulls scream sad abandon banking
high above the silt mouth where the mothering
sea pushes wearily lapping up
the last gift of the land.

The tide drags weed, the sea's
sore knees breed my wandering
upshore along an elbow of sand to gather
shark's-purse, washed shells, sailor's baubles, driftwood
eaten smooth
                soul white, and bluebottles

hover above the massive tunnelling waste-pipes
rust-crusted. Knives cut bait,
reefer smokers cast their ragged lines,
a tramp breaks bread, squatting to watch:
they say the glaucous mackerel

                    bite best

there because manshit
               has quality, is tasty

loosenest roots of the bowels, though
rubber disposals are more poetic
floating gently, wombless and flat, in a rock pool

did I wonder why
               sharks scuffle in the brown surf;
human limbs are the delicacies
               a careless
swimmer makes first-class offal

but the zenith sun of summer
who delivers details round the substance
  blood bone hair and fang:
where I am standing dumb my slim
shadow is quiet as a bottom circle
dark, composed, unhaloed—

               pared to trueness

The Shapes of Fear   *Richard Ntiru*

Like an arrested breath
when breathing makes silence imperfect
and the ear cannot differentiate
between the conspiratorial whispers and the wind's singing

a twig in the courtyard snaps
and the report of a gun is understood

Like the suspended step
when a mouldy piece of wood lies across the path
and the wary eye cannot separate
the snake supple slipperiness from the clumsy presence

the lone traveller sees the mirage on the road
and thinks again of Noah and the Flood

Like the drawn vacuum moment
when the inmate half-expectantly says Karibu
and the eye relieves the ear
to welcome the caller who does not enter

the late homecomer sees Baringa* at night
and suspects assassins all along the path

Like the timid child's time
between the deed and the

between the incidental slip of the tongue
and the roaring presence of the harsh mother
a loose pane falls from its frame
and the tenant has to look for a new house

Like this and so much more
in this nauseating odour of human mockery . . .

Lenrie Peters

On a wet September morning
    When vultures hate themselves
On the beach, against the flooded moorage
    Along the rock shelves

* A personification of the fear-causing illusions experienced on a
dark night.

Where sea-gulls lay their eggs.
  Half under the cracking waves
With sea-weed under my nails
  Where the coastline bends.
The sea was not the land's end.

The world under the sea
  The sea under the earth
The sky under the sea
  Were elemental changes of a world.
As the true life is death
  Which is the idea inside us
So distinction ends.
  The plagued centuries
In a weeping jelly-fish.
  The pebble that will be a crown
The moon reflected in a starfish.

My amputated feet
  Buried in soft sand
Within the blue shadows
  Were already prehistoric.
I tried to leap
  Out of shark's way
Far from the cutting teeth
  Thundering like the wave
Aimed at my vitals, not my feet

But they had planted roots
  Among the symbiosing weeds
Which issued from my feet
  Under the caressing current
Where disproportionate time
  Lulled in deep sleep.
I could not move;
  I say I could not move
My vegetable feet,

Only a silent yell
    Rang through time's corridors
To the farthest end
    Where the amoeba becomes
The fire, water and air.
    Where the primeval fruit still hangs.
So to the other end
    Where plants are but continents
Deep in the future
    That is darker and older
Than the past.

The echo burst inside me
    Like a great harmonic chord—
Violins of love and happy voices
    The pagan trumpet blast
Swamping the lamentation of the horn
    Then the heraldic drums
In slow crescendo rising
    Crashed through my senses
Into a new present
    Which is the future.

It was the music
    Floating on salt air
Mixture of ozone and fish, urea
    Boundless in all her forms
Like children's toys
    Which lifted me
Higher than myself
    From the palsied hand of destruction.
        In the new vibrations
            Came new awareness
        And care born of feeling
Fear, and the pestilence of thought
Was cradled in a wet pulsating stone.

How then the smell of fish
    The salted lips
Were like violets in a desert waste
    The rancid taste
Her priceless treasury of gems,
    Hot burning sands
Like the edentulous
    Sprouting palms.
The sea was the desert
    The wet was the dry
Here was there.
      All indistinguishable
Like the smell of
    Old men's trousers
From the Sunday joint.

Truth lay on the sea bed
    Black suffering on the land.
The sun raised gently her head
    As I lay buried on the sand.

Three Birds

Rabkarivelo

The bird of iron the bird of steel
that rent the morning clouds
and wanted to snatch the stars
is hiding shamefully
beyond day
in an unreal cave.

The bird of flesh the bird of feathers
that thrust a tunnel through the wind
in quest of the moon whom he saw in his dreams
hanging in the branches.
plunges like the evening
into a thicket of leaves.

But he who is without body
bewitches the guardian of skulls
with his stammering song.
He opens his sounding wings
hurries to pacify space
and only returns immortal.

Rabéarivelo

The black glassmaker
whose countless eyeballs none has ever seen
whose shoulders none has overlooked
that slave all clothed in pearls of glass
who is strong as Atlas
and who carried seven skies on his head
one would think that the vast river of clouds might carry him away,
the river in which his loincloth is already wet.

A thousand particles of glass
fall from his hands
but rebound towards his brow
shattered by mountains
where the winds are born.

And you are witness of his daily suffering
and of his endless task;
you watch his thunder-riddled agony
until the battlements of the East re-echo
the conches of the sea—
but you pity him no more
and do not even remember that his sufferings begin again
each time the sun capsizes.

Animistic Spells

Wole Soyinka

I

First you must
Walk among the faceless
Their feet are shod in earth
And dung
Caryatids in anterooms of night's inbirth

Shards strewn
On secret passages of night
Their creviced skin is dew
Inlaid, star-wells
For night of drought, for dearth of light

Hold
As they, bread as breath
Is held and spent, discarding
Weights of time
In clutching and possessing—yokes of death.

The quest
Is all, endless
Then home-coming
Respite
Before the gathering of the outward crest

II

Eyes
That grow as stamens need
A yeast of pollen. Shun
Visions
Of the unleavened, look sooner on the sun

III

Death
Embraces you and I
A twilight cone is

Meeting-place
The silent junction of the grey abyss

IV
The past
Dissolves in lacquered notes
Lips on woodwind, ears
Of grain
Swaying to echoes in a veil of rust

V
Incense
Of pines when a page
Is turned, woodsmoke
Rings
Across a thousand years to a bygone sage

VI
Fragments
We cannot hold, linger
Parings of intuition
Footsteps
Passing and re-passing the door of recognition

VII
Line
Of the withered bough
Hill and broken valleys
Dearth
On thirsty palm to furrows of the earth

VIII
Blood
When it is done—dearth
Of lines from palm to love
Light,
Springs, to patient wrinkles on the earth

IX

Links

Of dust, whitened rib
Of ghosts to flute
Home-coming
Moth-fingers hover on the new-laid crib.

X

Old moons
Set your crescent eyes
On bridges of my hands
Comb out
Manes of sea-wind on my tide-swept sands

XI

Seed
A bowl of dark unblemish
A chancel closed in forest
Silences
Repletion for earth's own regenerate need

A wind's
Dark mantle brushes past
A quiet prelude to the stir
Of germ
A cycle's ether sieve for pollen hair

Fall seeds
Then, to mineral hands
Flush out in your green
And gentle blades
Awaken minds and grow to cosmic shades

XII

Buried lakes
My feet, satanic cleft
Spring-divining feet have mined
Buried lakes
Calms in opal caverns of the mind

Incense-boat
Amber flare, a broken
Bolt awash in indigo
Sky and voice
Peace of light before the death token

Sough of wings
Moonsward on night, guides
To skyscapes of the mind
Unfettered
Now begins the flight on memory tides

XIII

Offerings
That cling to us teach
To give is to suffer
To share
A bitter foretaste of the death we bear

Altar-vessel
Of one skull shall bear
Offerings for the ascent
Multitudes
Shall dance on flesh remains of a cosmic dare

XIV

Three millet
Stalks. A tasselled crown
On a broken glass horizon
Weeds clogged
Their feet, winds came and blew them down

New ears arose
Lean lances through
A stubbed and mangled mound—
And this I saw—
Their grains were ripened closer to the ground.

Agony

there is no better key to dreams
than my name sang a bird
in a lake of blood
the sea danced alongside
dressed in blue-jeans
blowing the squalling gulls to bits

a black boatman
who claimed to know the stars
said he could cure with the mud of his sad eyes
the lepers of their leprosy
if a tonic love would unloose his arms

my name is key to dreams
I am not leprous
take me across this river before you speak my name -
and your arms will be unloosed

I hold the singing oar
where is this river I must cross
is it that lake of blood

follow me
close your eyes
think of the moon
contemplate my river
and let us cross

the man and the bird sang
steered three days three nights to cross
the dirty bed of a river

listen
the wave rocks the boatman
he sleeps
he dreams

a charnel house offers a feast
where his bowels are eaten first
then his arms then his memory

where the putrid bodies eat each other
by the glimmer of fire-flies
which each carries at his temples
striving to resemble the christian god

there where they drink the slow song of the nightingale

one innocent pities his legs
scrapes from the bowl of ebony-wood
the last scrap of his memory
rope dancer on the thread
of low-water mark

He knows the love which opposes his pain
the nightmares of the boatman in his troubled sleep
the wings of the birds who float their anthem
and who row too happily over the singing water

on the far bank the plain comes to drink
with its troops of wild grasses
bellowing their thirst in a tropical rhythm
while the peevish sun stabs at them

the sun pricks the side of the fisherman
his swords all newly forged

all newly tempered
with blood
and this blood oozes from the earth
and trickles from the sky
on a night of yellow rain

the boatman tells his name to the quail

no my name is key to dreams
I am not leprous
quail is not my name
do not die awaiting me

I am your soul farewell
my dark body farewell
your arms will unloose themselves
I am not leprous

do not die awaiting me
arms opened in a cross

IV
Black Thoughts

Expelled

Jared Angira

We had traded in this market competitively perfect
till you came, in the boat, and polished goodwill
approval from high order
all pepper differentials, denied flag-bearers

and cut our ribs, dried our cows
the vaccine from the lake
burst the cowshed, the draught you brought
planted on the market place, the tree of memory

I had no safe locket to keep my records
when Sodom burnt, and Gomorrah fell
the debtors' records blared
the creditors tapped my rusty door

My tears flowed to flooded streams
and sources the rivulets from my human lake
from my veins, my heart, my whole
disposition of the last penny
the last sight of my fishing-net

Everyone avoids my path; I avoid death's too
pursuit in a dark circus
the floating garden in a gale
plants reject sea water, the sea water rejects me
I have nothing to reject
the broken line runs across my face

The auctioneer will gong his hammer
for the goods left behind.

Daughter of the Low Land

Peter Anyang'-Nyong'O

After I have communed with them
With dead men's ideas
"Nya dyang'" comes to me
With accusing persuasion:
    "Come, 'wuod twon',
      My activities are vital."

I do not let my testicles
Be crushed when I am wide awake
By the ghosts of an alien clan
In the half-lighted book-cave;
No!
When I sheathe the family spear
And unfeather the poison-horned arrow;
When I expose the daughter of the low land
To village gossip and contempt:
Then the books that I read
Smash my testicles in my sleep!

My testicles
Have not been smashed
By heavy books!
    "Ocol,
      Drink from the roots;
      You were first wedded to me
      And then to Plato
      And Aristotle."

I do not sit there
In that forest
Of dead men's heads
Letting their heavy tongues—
Like "rungus"—
Butt my balls to wind's dust;
No!
Like the emissary

Of a semi-famished land,
Or the scout of a belligerent army,
I brew with the enemy
And drink with my people.

And when I return home
To the daughter of the brave one,
The yeast from the low land
Makes my manhood
Rise.

Black Mother

Viriato da Cruz

Your presence, mother, is the living drama of a race
drama of flesh and blood
which Life has written with the pen of centuries.

Through your voice

Voices from the cane plantations,
the paddy fields, the coffee farms,
the silk works, the
cotton fields
Voices from plantations in Virginia
from farms in the Carolinas
Alabama
Cuba
Brazil
Voices from Brazilian sugar plants,
from the tonga drums, from the
pampas, from factories,
Voices from Harlem District South,
voices from slum locations,
Voices wailing blues going up the
Mississippi, echoing from rail road wagons.
Voices weeping with Carrother's voice
"Lord God what will have we done"

Voice of all voices in the proud voice
        of Langston
in the beautiful voice of Guillen . . .

Through your back

Gleaming backs beneath the world's strongest suns
Gleaming backs making fertile with their blood
        working soft with their sweat
        the world's richest soils
Gleaming (ai, the colour of those backs . . .)
Gleaming backs twisted on the torso
        hanging from the gallows, struck down by Lynch
Gleaming backs (ah, how they gleam, those backs)
Revived with Zumbi, raised up with Toussaint
Gleaming backs
they gleam, they gleam, drummers of jazz
they break, they break the fetters of the soul
escape soul on the wings of music
. . . of sunlight, of the sun, immortal, fecund
        and beautiful

Through your lap, mother

Rocking those other people
spoilt by the voice of tenderness
and fed on your sustaining milk,
        the good of poetry
        of music, of rhythm and gracefulness,
sacred poets and wise men . .
These people have no sons
for these which are born like wild beasts,
self generated, different things
are rather the sons of disgrace:
the hoe is their plaything
slave labour—their recreation . . .

I see oceans of grief
lit by the setting sun, landscapes,
violet landscapes
dramas of Cain and Japheth.
But I see as well (oh if I see . . .)
I see as well how the light robbed from your
     eyes now glows
demoniacal temptress—like Certainty
glittering steadily—like Hope
in us, your other sons
making, forming, announcing
the day of humanity
THE DAY OF HUMANITY.

I Thank You God

Bernard Dadié

I thank you God for creating me black,
For making of me
Porter of all sorrows,
Setting on my head
The World.
I wear the Centaur's hide
And I have carried the World since the first morning.

White is a colour for special occasions
Black the colour for every day
And I have carried the World since the first evening.

I am glad
Of the shape of my head
Made to carry the World,
Content
With the shape of my nose
That must snuff every wind of the World
Pleased
With the shape of my legs
Ready to run all the heats of the World.

84

I thank you God for creating me black
For making of me
Porter of all sorrows.

Thirty-six swords have pierced my heart.
Thirty-six fires have burnt my body.
And my blood on all calvaries has reddened the snow,
And my blood at every dawn has reddened all nature.

Still I am
Glad to carry the World,
Glad of my short arms
   of my long arms
      of the thickness of my lips.

I thank you God for creating me black.
White is a colour for special occasions
Black the colour for every day
And I have carried the World since the dawn of time.
And my laugh over the World, through the night, creates the Day.

I thank you God for creating me black.

If You Want to Know Me

Noémia de Sousa

If you want to know me
examine with careful eyes
this bit of black wood
which some unknown Makonde brother
cut and carved
with his inspired hands
in the distant lands of the North.

This is what I am
empty sockets despairing of possessing life
a mouth torn open in an anguished wound
huge hands outspread

and raised in imprecation and in threat
a body tattooed with wounds seen and unseen
from the harsh whipstrokes of slavery
tortured and magnificent
proud and mysterious
Africa from head to foot
This is what I am.

If you want to understand me
come, bend over this soul of Africa
in the black dockworker's groans
the Chope's frenzied dances
the Changanas' rebellion
in the strange sadness which flows
from an African song, through the night.

And ask no more
to know me
for I'm nothing but a shell of flesh
where Africa's revolt congealed
its cry pregnant with hope.

Sell-Out

David Diop

Brother—teeth flashing in the cant of compliments
Brother—gold-rimmed glasses
Across eyes that go blue at a word from the Master
Poor brother in your silk-lined tuxedo
Chatter and whisper and swagger through condescending
        drawing-rooms
We pity you
The sun of your land is no more than a shadow
Across the calm brow of a civilized man
And your grandmother's hut
Reddens a face whited by the bowing and
Scraping of years
But when you are sick of the words as sounding and empty

As the cash-box perched on your shoulders
You will tread the African earth bitter and red
And your restless steps will be to the rhythm of this tormented
    refrain
Alone here alone how all alone I feel!

Listen Comrades

David Diop

Listen comrades of the struggling centuries
To the keen clamour of the Negro from Africa to the Americas
They have killed Mamba
As they killed the seven of Martinsville
Or the Madagascan down there in the pale light on the prisons
He held in his look comrades
The warm faith of a heart without anguish
And his smile despite agony
Despite the wounds of his broken body
Kept the bright colours of a bouquet of hope
It is true that they have killed Mamba with his white hairs
Who ten times poured forth for us milk and light
I feel his mouth on my dreams
And the peaceful tremor of his breast
And I am lost again
Like a plant torn from the maternal bosom
But no
For there rings out higher than my sorrows
Purer than the morning where the wild beast wakes
The cry of a hundred people smashing their cells
And my blood long held in exile
The blood they hoped to snare in a circle of words
Rediscovers the fervour that scatters the mists
Listen comrades of the struggling centuries
To the keen clamour of the Negro from Africa to the Americas
It is the sign of the dawn
The sign of brotherhood which comes to nourish the dreams of men.

Anti-Grace

Paulin Joachim

I call anti-grace
first the offering up of life
as an unending battle waged to bring light
(in this divided province where nothing happens
where no road goes up a mountain
where the sun itself now never rises out of the hollow of the sea)
into this nethermost dungeon where history has stopped breathing
the only inhabitants now a clutch of mindless oysters
who in their perpetual condition of iodized rapture
allow themselves to be consumed in white butter

anti-grace
a life dismal and congealed
like an enormous hernia drooping from a tripe-stall
I call anti-grace
that epileptic pendulum sprung from the Angel's malice
swinging back and forth
passing into the sun and passing into the shade
powerless to shatter History
and to reach the privileged rock where the Spirit has set
his seed which binds and loosens
powerless to rise from its offence

anti-grace
those pincers deep at the roots of being
at the height of love
the full armour of the man plundered in the dawns
his portion filched his leap forbidden
his blue sky confiscated by apostates
yet I had dreamed of a life pearl-white
like the first smoke of morning in the village sky
I dreamed of being born with a bugle at the heart
so that every impulse should be unbroken

I call anti-grace
that life of scraps and little words
drawing doubt to your skin at the moment of leaping

I dreamed of an engine
pulling full steam on its train of stars
reckoning without the anti-grace
that condemns me to a long expiring loneliness
on the straw of agricultural shows
I had dreamed before I was born of being a prince not a peasant

I call anti-grace
my face out of hell considered undesirable on the Broadway of
    pleasure
like a curt acknowledgment of some disgrace
the typhoon of loving clinched to the miner's slow toil
and the world around still insists on spelling out my shame
while I look so hard that I lose sight of it

anti-grace
special pleading never winding its winding up up
solo turn of an ageing star who will never leave me
the past engulfed under torrents of words
and these shadows instead of men at the crossroads of reckoning
leave me to cry I have no more speech
the master organists the enemies of polyphony
have interlined my now illegible speech
to be born without pills for sea-sickness
is what I call anti-grace
banana skins under foot
for an unending slalom down the slopes of life
and this performance is continuous
for the race has risen up again greater and greater
since she made her womb fertile under the hatches of the slave ships

and if grace exists and if love is rustproof
if grace hears me
let her bring to sight at last
on the palette where since the first day I have ground the colours of
    my destiny
the cornaline glints where my race standing
will read the premonishing signals of triumphs to come.

Notes from No Sanctuary

Keorapetse Kgositsile

I

There are no sanctuaries
except in purposeful action;
I could say to my child,
There are wounds deeper
than flesh. Deeper and more
concrete than belief in some god
who would imprison your eye
in the sterile sky instead of
thrusting it on the piece of earth
you walk everyday and say,
Reclaim it.

But I let it pass since
it is really about knowing today and how.
This is what it has come to. Daughters
and sons are born now and could ask,
you know: Knowing your impotence why
did you bring me here?

I could say:
Life is the unarguable referent.
What you know is merely a point
of departure. So let's move. But we have
been dead so long and *continue*. There will
be no songs this year. We no longer
sing. Except perhaps some hideous
gibberish like james brown making believe
he is american or beautiful or proud. Or
some fool's reference to allah who, like
jehovah, never gave a two-bit shit about niggers.

I could say, like Masekela,
We are in jail here. Which is
to say, We have done nothing.
I could say, . . . but see,

What difference does it make
as long as we eat white shit?
not matter what it is wrapped up in!

2

How many deaths and specific
how or when ago was it
the rememberer said, where
to go is what to do?

   Still we talk *somuch*!

And cold black hustlers of my generation claw
their way into the whitenesses of their desire
and purpose. Here a slave's groan and shudder
is a commodity the hustler peddles newly-wrapped
in. *brother, sister, revolution, power to the people* . . .

   So now having spoken our time or referent,
   a people's soul gangrened to impotence,
   all the obscene black&whitetogether kosher
   shit of mystified apes . . . Where then is
   the authentic song? The determined
   upagainstthewallmotherfucker act?

   So say you say you float above
   this menace, having violently tasted
   white shit past the depths of any
   word you know. Say you float above
   the dollar-green eye of the hustler whose
   purpose is cloaked in dashikis and glib
   statements about revolution.

        Say you float
untouchably above this menace, does
your purpose, if there be one, propose
to be less impotent than this poem?

Home-Coming Son

Look where you walk unholy stranger
This is the land of the eighth harmony
In the rainbow: Black.
It is the dark side of the moon
Brought to light
This is the canvas of God's master stroke.

Out, of your foreign outfit unholy stranger
Feel part of the great work of art
Walk in peace, walk alone, walk tall,
Walk free, walk naked
Let the feelers of your mother land
Caress your bare feet
Let Her breath kiss your naked body.

But watch, watch where you walk forgotten stranger
This is the very depth of your roots: Black.
Where the tom-toms of your fathers vibrated
In the fearful silence of the valleys
Shook, in the colossus bodies of the mountains
Hummed, in the deep chest of the jungles.
Walk proud.

Watch, listen to the calls of the ancestral spirits prodigal son
To the call of the long awaited soil
They welcome you home, home. In the song of birds
You hear your suspended family name
The winds whisper the golden names of your tribal warriors
The fresh breeze blown onto your nostrils
Floats their bones turned to dust.
Walk tall. The spirits welcome
Their lost-son returned.

Watch, and out of your foreign outfit brother
Feel part of the work of art
Walk in . . . . in rhythm, walk tall

Walk free, walk naked.
Let the roots of your motherland caress your body
Let the naked skin absorb the home-sun and shine e'...y.

Attention   *Mindelense*

The lights of the city glide within me
but do not pierce through me with their glitter
deep in me there still persists the black depths
of the black history I hear singing

I have heard of blood that ran in torrents
and of the whip that cracked a thousand times,
of the white man who stood guard on the slaves,
sparks in his eyes and thunder in his voice.

We here are the children of a dense night
which is shattered in place by strange cries
rages suppressed for many hundred years
today are globules of our own red blood.

Oh wonderful things, oh cities of light
you nights do not keep company with me
within me there still remains the black bass
of the black history I hear singing.

You Laughed and Laughed and Laughed   *Gabriel Okara*

In your ears my song
is motor car misfiring
stopping with a choking cough;
and you laughed and laughed and laughed.

In your eyes my ante-
natal walk was inhuman passing
your "omnivorous understanding"
and you laughed and laughed and laughed.

You laughed at my song
you laughed at my walk.

Then I danced my magic dance
to the rhythm of talking
drums pleading, but you shut your
eyes and laughed and laughed and laughed.

And then I opened my mystic
inside wide like
the sky, instead you entered your
car and laughed and laughed and laughed.

You laughed at my dance
you laughed at my inside.

You laughed and laughed and laughed.
But your laughter was ice-block
laughter and it froze your inside froze
your voice froze your ears
froze your eyes and froze your tongue.

And now it's my turn to laugh;
but my laughter is not
ice-block laughter. For I
know not cars, know not ice-blocks.

My laughter is the fire
of the eye of the sky, the fire
of the earth, the fire of the air
the fire of the seas and the
river fishes animals trees
and it thawed your inside,
thawed your voice, thawed your
ears, thawed your eyes, and
thawed your tongue.

So a meek wonder held
your shadow and you whispered:
"Why so?"
And I answered:
"Because my fathers and I
are owned by the living
warmth of the earth
through our naked feet."

Tomatoes   *Yambo Ouologuem*

People think I'm a cannibal
But you know what people say

People see I've got red gums but who has
White ones
Up the tomatoes

People say there are not nearly so many tourists
Now
But you know
This isn't America and nobody
Has the money

People think it's my fault and are scared
But look
My teeth are white not red
I've not eaten anybody

People are rotten they say I scoff
Baked tourists
Or maybe grilled
Baked or grilled was my order
They don't say anything just keep looking uneasily at my gums
Up the tomatoes

Everyone knows in an agricultural country there's agriculture
Up the vegetables

Everyone knows that vegetables
Well you can't live on the vegetables you grow
And that I'm quite well developed for someone underdeveloped
Miserable scum living off the tourists
Down with my teeth

People suddenly surrounded me
Tied me up
Threw me down
At the feet of justice
Cannibal or not cannibal
Answer

Ah you think you're so clever
So proud of yourself

Well we'll see I'm going to settle your account
Have you anything to say
Before you are sentenced to death

I shouted Up the tomatoes

People are rotten and women curious you know
There was one of these in the curious circle
In her rasping voice sort of bubbling like a saucepan
With a hole in it
Shrieked
Slit open his belly
I'm sure father is still inside

There weren't any knives
Naturally enough among the vegetarians
Of the western world
So they got a Gillette blade
And carefully
Slit
Slat
Plop
Slit open my belly

Inside flourishing rows of tomatoes
Watered by streams of palm wine
Up the tomatoes

Murders

L. S. Senghor

They are lying there along the captured roads, along the roads of
disaster
Slender poplars, statues of the sombre gods wrapped in long
golden cloaks
The prisoners from Senegal lie like lengthened shadows across
the soil of France.

In vain they have chopped down your laughter, and the darker
flower of your flesh
You are the flower of the foremost beauty in stark absence of
flowers
Black flower and solemn smile, diamond time out of mind.
You are the clay and the plasma of the world's virid spring
Flesh you are of the first couple, the fertile belly, milk and
sperm
You are the sacred fecundity of the bright paradise gardens

And the incoercible forest, victor over fire and thunder.
The immense song of your blood will conquer machines and
mortars
The pulse of your speech, lies and sophistry
No hate your heart without hate, no guile your heart without
guile.
Black Martyrs O undying race, give me leave to say the words
which will forgive.

Letter to a Poet   *L. S. Senghor*
to Aimé Césaire

To the Brother I love and the friend, my blunt, fraternal greeting!
The black gulls, the far-travelling canoe-masters have brought
    me some taste of your news
Mingled with spices, with the fragrant sounds of the Rivers of
    the South and the Islands.
They have told of your standing, the prominence of your
    forehead and the flower of your subtle lips
They say that your disciples are a hive of silence, a peacock's
    fan
And till the moon's rising you hold them, breathless and keen.
Is it your perfume of fabulous fruits or the bright wake behind
    you at height of noon?
So many wives dark-skinned as sapodilla in the harem of your
    mind!

Across the years it holds me, the live coal,
Under the ash of your eyelids, your music we reached out
    hands and hearts to long ago.
Can you forget your nobility, which is to sing
The Ancestors the Princes the Gods (they are not flowers nor
    drops of dew)?
It was your duty to offer the Spirits white fruits from your
    garden
(You ate only flour of fine millet, ground from the same year's
    harvest)
Stealing not a single petal to sweeten your mouth.
At the bottom of the well of my memory, I touch
Your face and there draw water to freshen my long regret.
Royally you lie at length, propping your elbow on the cushion
    of a bright hill,
And the earth labours gently under the weight of your couch
In the flooded plains the drums beat out your song, and your
    verse is the breathing of the night and the distant sea.
You sang the Ancestors and the legitimate princes
You plucked out of the sky a star for a rhyme

Syncopating the rhythm; at your bare feet the poor cast down as
    mats the earnings of a year
And the women cast down at your bare feet their hearts of
    amber and the dance you dragged from their souls.

My friend my friend—O! you will come back you will come back!
I will wait for you—I have given the message to the master of
    the cutter—under the kaicedrat.
You will come back at the feast of the first fruits. When the
    sweetness of evening smokes on the roofs as the sun declines
And the athletes parade their youth, decked like bridegrooms, it
    is fitting that you should come.

African Communion   *Tom Simpson*

They came concealed in ceremonial robes:
HIC EST ENIM CORPUS MEUM.
White robes, beautifully bright robes:
Behold, your new God!
But this new God was a jealous God,
And righteous was his jealousy;
He was pure,
White,
Abstract,
Singular,
Universal;
He would suffer no toleration of black gods,
Impure gods,
Gods of darkness and not of light.
The light was shone in the darkness,
And the black gods were sent to a black, ashy death.

Around the African body was draped the new robe;
A skin, white,
Stripped from the man they called their God.
A skin stripped from the man they sacrificed to their selves.

But the skin bore a parasite,
And it ate of the African body
As white eats of black,
As white eats of Christ's black death,
To hide the guilt of their sin,
To begin the ceremony of the communion
Which was their division.
"Take you and eat of this, for this is my body."

The unleaven wafer was taken and eaten,
And it nourished the Saviours who had brought
   Africa its Salvation.

V
Captivity

Cold

the clammy cement
sucks our naked feet

a rheumy yellow bulb
lights a damp grey wall

the stubbled grass
wet with three o'clock dew
is black with glittery edges;

we sit on the concrete,
stuff with our fingers
the sugarless pap
into our mouths

then labour erect;

form lines;

steel ourselves into fortitude
or accept an image of ourselves
numb with resigned acceptance;

the grizzled senior warden comments:
"Things like these
I have no time for;

they are worse than rats;
you can only shoot them."

Overhead
the large frosty glitter of the stars
the Southern Cross flowering low;

the chains on our ankles
and wrists

that pair us together
jangle

glitter.

We begin to mov
 awkwardly.

Colesberg: en route to Robben Island

Letters to Martha   *Dennis Brutus*

2
One learns quite soon
that nails and screws
and other sizeable bits of metal
must be handed in;

and seeing them shaped and sharpened
one is chilled, appalled
to see how vicious it can be
—this simple, useful bit of steel:

and when these knives suddenly flash
—produced perhaps from some disciplined anus—
one grasps at once the steel-bright horror
in the morning air
and how soft and vulnerable is naked flesh.

4
Particularly in a single cell
but even in sections
the religious sense asserts itself;

perhaps a childhood habit of nightly prayers
the accessibility of Bibles,
or awareness of the proximity of death:

and of course, it is a currency—
pietistic expressions can purchase favours
and it is a way of suggesting reformation
(which can procure promotion);

and the resort of the weak
is to invoke divine revenge
against a rampaging injustice;

but in the grey silence of the empty afternoons
it is not uncommon
to find oneself talking to God.

5

In the greyness of isolated time
which shafts down into the echoing mind,
wraiths appear, and whispers of horrors
that people the labyrinth of self.

Coprophilism; necrophilism; fellatio;
penis-amputation;
and in this gibbering society
hooting for recognition as one's other selves
suicide, self-damnation, walks
if not a companionable ghost
then a familiar familiar,
a doppelgänger
not to be shaken off.

6

Two men I knew specifically
among many cases:
their reactions were enormously different
but a tense thought lay at the bottom of each
and for both there was danger and fear and pain—
drama.

One simply gave up smoking
knowing he could be bribed
and hedged his mind with romantic fantasies
of beautiful marriageable daughters;

the other sought escape
in fainting fits and asthmas
and finally fled into insanity:

so great the pressures to enforce sodomy.

Letter from Pretoria Central Prison   *Arthur Nortje*

The bell wakes me at 6 in the pale spring dawn
with the familiar rumble of the guts negotiating
murky corridors that smell of bodies. My eyes
find salutary the insurgent light of distances.
Waterdrops rain crystal cold, my wet
face in ascent from an iron basin
greets its rifled shadow in the doorway.

They walk us to the workshop. I am eminent,
the blacksmith of the block: these active hours
fly like sparks in the furnace, I hammer metals
with zest letting the sweating muscles
forge a forgetfulness of worlds more magnetic.
The heart, being at rest, life peaceable,
your words filter softly through my fibres.

Taken care of, in no way am I unhappy,
being changed to neutral. You must decide
today, tomorrow, bear responsibility,
take gaps in pavement crowds, refine ideas.
Our food we get on time. Most evenings
I read books, Jane Austen
for elegance, agreeableness (Persuasion).

Trees are green beyond the wall, leaves through the mesh
are cool in sunshine
among the monastic white flowers of spring that floats
prematurely across the exercise yard, a square
of the cleanest stone I have ever walked on.
Sentinels smoke in their boxes, the wisps
curling lovely through the barbed wire.

Also music and cinema, yesterday double feature.
At 4 pm it's back to the cell, don't laugh
to hear how accustomed one becomes. You spoke
of hospital treatment—I see the smart nurses
bringing you grapefruit and tea—good
luck to the troublesome kidney.
Sorry there's no more space. But date your reply.

August 1966

Purgatory

Wole Soyinka

Wall of flagellation to the South
Strokes of justice slice a festive air—
It is the day of reckoning

In puppet cast: first, by law compelled
The surgeon, ether primed for the ordeal.
Next, a cardboard row of gaolers, eyelids
Of glue—the observation squad. And:
Hero of the piece, a towering shade across
The prostrate villain, cuts a trial swathe
In air, nostalgic for the thumbscrew
Rack and nail extractors—alas, all
Good things shall pass away—he adapts
To the regulation cane. Stage props:
Bench for a naked body, crusted towel,
Pail of antiseptic yellow to impart
Wet timbres to dry measures of the Law.

The circus comes to circus town
A freak show comes to freaks
And ancient pageant to divert
Archetypes of Purgatorio

For here the mad commingle with the damned.
Epileptics, seers and visionaries
Addicts of unknown addictions, soulmates
To the vegetable soul, and grey
Companions to the ghosts of landmarks
Trudging the lifelong road to a dread
Judicial sentence

And some have walked to the edge of the valley
Of the shadow; and, at a faint stir in memories
Long faded to the moment of the miracle of reprieve
To a knowledge of rebirth and a promise of tomorrows
And tomorrows and an ever beginning of tomorrows
The mind retreats behind a calloused shelter
Of walls, self-sensor on the freedom of remembrance
Tempering visions of opaque masonry, to rings
Of iron spikes, a peace of refuge passionless
And comfort of a gelded sanity.

Weaned from the moment of death, the miracle
Dulled, their minds dissolve in vagueness, a look
Empty as all thoughts are featureless which
Plunge to that lone abyss—And
Had it there ended? Had it all ended, there
Even in the valley of the shadow of Night?

VI
Compatriot

No Coffin, No Grave   *Jared Angira*

He was buried without a coffin
without a grave
the scavengers performed the post-mortem
in the open mortuary
without sterilized knives
in front of the night club

stuttering rifles put up
the gun salute of the day
that was a state burial anyway
the car knelt
the red plate wept, wrapped itself into blood its master's

the diary revealed to the sea
the rain anchored there at last
isn't our flag red, black, and white?
so he wrapped himself well

who could signal yellow
when we had to leave politics to the experts
and brood on books
brood on hunger
and schoolgirls
grumble under the black pot
sleep under torn mosquito net
and let lice lick our intestines
the lord of the bar, money speaks madam
woman magnet, money speaks madam
we only cover the stinking darkness
of the cave of our mouths
and ask our father who is in hell to judge him
the quick and the good.

Well, his diary, submarine of the Third World War
showed he wished
to be buried in a gold-laden coffin

like a VIP
under the jacaranda tree beside his palace
a shelter for his grave
and much beer for the funeral party

anyway one noisy pupil suggested we bring
tractors and plough the land.

Nightsong City

Dennis Brutus

Sleep well, my love, sleep well:
the harbour lights glaze over restless docks,
police cars cockroach through the tunnel streets;

from the shanties creaking iron-sheets
violence like a bug-infested rag is tossed
and fear is immanent as sound in the wind-swung bell;

the long day's anger pants from sand and rocks;
but for this breathing night at least,
my land, my love, sleep well.

The Casualties
to Chinua Achebe

J. P. Clark

The casualties are not only those who are dead;
They are well out of it.
The casualties are not only those who are wounded,
Though they await burial by instalment.
The casualties are not only those who have lost
Persons or property, hard as it is
To grope for a touch that some
May not know is not there.
The casualties are not only those led away by-night;
The cell is a cruel place, sometimes a haven,
Nowhere as absolute as the grave.

The casualties are not only those who started
A fire and now cannot put it out. Thousands
Are burning that had no say in the matter.
The casualties are not only those who escaping
The shattered shell become prisoners in
A fortress of falling walls.

The casualties are many, and a good number well
Outside the scenes of ravage and wreck;
They are the emissaries of rift,
So smug in smoke-rooms they haunt abroad,
They do not see the funeral piles
At home eating up the forests.
They are the wandering minstrels who, beating on
The drums of the human heart, draw the world
Into a dance with rites it does not know

The drums overwhelm the guns . . .

Caught in the clash of counter claims and charges
When not in the niche others have left,
We fall,
All casualties of the war,
Because we cannot hear each other speak,
Because eyes have ceased to see the face from the crowd,
Because whether we know or
Do not know the extent of wrong on all sides,
We are characters now other than before
The war began, the stay-at-home unsettled
By taxes and rumours, the looters for office
And wares, fearful everyday the owners may return
We are all casualties,
All sagging as are
The cases celebrated for kwashiorkc.,
The unforeseen camp-follower of not just our war.

Mamparra M'gaiza*

José Craveirinha

The cattle is selected
counted, marked
and gets on the train, stupid cattle.

In the pen
the females stay behind
to breed new cattle.

The train is back from "migoudini"**
and they come rotten with diseases, the old cattle of Africa
oh, and they've lost their heads, these cattle "m'gaiza"

Come and see
the sold cattle have lost their heads
my god of my land
the sold cattle have lost their heads.

Again
the cattle is selected, marked
and the train is ready to take away meek cattle

Stupid cattle
mine cattle
cattle of Africa, marked and sold.

* M'gaiza (also magaiça) is a Mozambican expression for a man just
returned from the mines, his pockets full of money and his health
broken.
** Dialect for the mines.

Upheaval
Mbella Sonne Dipoko

Three nights in a single file sobbed in the rain
As in the tyrant's heart a hope shivered
Hating the time to come.

His eyes were only particles of light
Tiny petals on the mourner's robes
As in the horses of the castle neighed
And cats begged for wings.
On the sinking throne a rat sat waiting its turn to die.

Rulers
Mbella Sonne Dipoko

This is a rainy night.
Rulers unroll scrolls of wretched landscapes
And boast and drink and dance under chandeliers
In castles threatened like pleasure boats in a furious ocean.
They are like insects that dance around street lamps
Looming in the fog of a stormy sky.

This is a seismic night;
Water-divide hills sink into valleys
And rivers flow backwards.
Our faces and farms drip with salt water from the flooded ocean.

But while our hope splits like lips in winter
We must seek the reticent sea-gull before it drowns
Mourned by stray crows.

Such is the fate of the wicked kingdom
Governed by gorgeous parrots.

Goodbye, Europeans

J. R. D. A. Dubreka

Goodbye, Europeans
And without a grudge
I, myself, am not offended
Goodbye, every one to his own home
Without any fuss
Goodbye provided you disturb us no more
Let him follow you
He who believes you indispensable.

The Struggle

Charles Kabuto Kabuye

we live in each other's pockets,
envying our neighbours' cooking pots,
while we leave our toes in our shoes
to be gnawed at by little ticklish bugs
of laziness, drug-addiction and drunkenness.

in the beer bars we struggle to impress,
while others work to suppress us,
treating us like little flies and fleas
which produce noises only to be ignored.

who called you great, you?
he meant you're a goat.
they call me clever
saying I'm a bin-cover,
a rubbish tip in the city heap.

then a city councillor calls me
to the King's Palace, I smile with content,
but there, I am no more than a common beggar
smelling of common-place liquor.
you dress in morning suit with a bow tie,
but you pass for a beggar

drinking local punch seated on a bench,
not in the palace, but in the commoners' trench:
you were in a dream in a lousy bed.

Metamorphosis

Amin Kassam

two hours ago
he sauntered in
ordinary man
purchased a ticket
two hours ago
anonymous in the queue
unnoticed
slouched to his seat

now
he swaggers
arrogant
the light of battle in his eyes
handsome
debonair
unruffled under awe-struck stares
feels strength
flowing
feels too the beretta
under his armpit.

cruel lips
bear the stamp of ruthlessness

beware
double-o-seven
has licence to kill
when how whom
he chooses!

Mother Earth
or the Folly of National Boundaries

Mazisi Kunene

Why should those at the end of the earth
Not drink from the same calabash
And build their homes in the valley of the earth
And together grow with our children?

The Motoka

Theo Luzuka

You see that Benz sitting at the rich's end?
Ha! That motoka is motoka
It belongs to the Minister for Fairness
Who yesterday was loaded with a doctorate
At Makerere with whisky and I don't know what
Plus I hear the literate thighs of an undergraduate.

You see those market women gaping their mouths?
The glory of its inside has robbed them of words,
I tell you the feather seats the gold steering
The TV the radio station the gear!
He can converse with all world presidents
While driving in the back seat with his darly
Between his legs without the driver seeing a thing! ha! ha! h
Look at the driver chasing the children away
They want to see the pistol in the door pocket
Or the button that lets out bullets from the machine
Through the eyes of the car-sshhhhhhhhhhhhhhhhhh!
Let's not talk about it.

But I tell you that motoka can run
It sails like a lyato, speeds like a swallow
And doesn't know anyone stupid on its way
The other day I heard—
But look at its behind, that mother of twins!

A-ah! That motoka is motoka
You just wait, I'll tell you more
But let me first sell my tomatoes.

Night

Agostinho Neto

I live
in the dark quarters of the world
without light, nor life.

Anxious to live,
I walk in the streets
feeling my way
leaning into my shapeless dreams,
stumbling into servitude.
  —Dark quarters,
   worlds of wretchedness
where the will is watered down
and men
are confused with things.

I walk, lurching
through the unlit
unknown streets crowded
with mystery and terror,
I, arm in arm with ghosts.
And the night too is dark.

<u>Kinaxixi</u>

Agostinho Neto

I was glad to sit down
on a bench in Kinaxixi
at six o'clock of a hot evening
and just sit there . . .

Someone would come
maybe

to sit beside me

And I would see the black faces
of the people going uptown
in no hurry
expressing absence in the
jumbled Kimbundu they conversed in.

I would see the tired footsteps
of the servants whose fathers also are servants
looking for love here, glory there, wanting
something more than drunkenness in every
alcohol

Neither happiness nor hate

After the sun had set
lights would be turned on and I
would wander off
thinking that our life after all is simple
too simple
for anyone who is tired and still has to walk.

Mood of the Years

Richard Ntiru

The People's perspective reporter's face arrives,
an indeterminate watershed between the legendary world
of what might have been and the hypothetical world
of what will probably be.
Assignment: to divine from Korokoto-Magambo
what seed he's cast on the fresh Timescape
and what fruit he'll reap from the season's Tree.

Korokoto-Magambo's hands unite in a mystical clasp,
And thus his shaggy moustache begins to enchant:
Though I've not sown on the new Timescape,
I'll join the chorus in the reapers' song—
Who dare discriminate in the feast of harvests?

My horizon being near, the quest shall be easier.
Among the unaligned, uncommitted,
I'll not wholly lack ideological commitment.
I'll chant the Charter in the reaper's song—
Who dare discriminate in the feast of harvests?

My leisure being limited, my polish shall be spare.
Among the illiterate, uneducated,
I'll show some symptoms of modern civilization.
I'll sing my literacy certificate in the reapers' song—
Who dare discriminate in the feast of harvests?

My house being small, the roof shall be lower.
Among the poor agrarian populace,
I'll not lack a shilling to share a bottle of waragi.
I'll applaud the Chief of Foreign Money in the reapers' song—
Who dare discriminate in the feast of harvests?

My will being weak, my ambition to be meek.
Among the masses nibbling at the edge of stale ideas,
I'll need no power to wield the tribes.
I'll sing to the tune of Gowon's gun in the reapers' song—
Who dare discriminate in the feast of harvests?

My morals being flexible, my stance to be miscible.
Among the rabble chasing the pleasure of the moment,
I'll not lack the suave of a younging society.
I'll dance to the palpitations of teenage rhythms in the reapers'
    song—
Who dare discriminate in the feast of harvests?

My brains being few, my part to be faceless.
Among the analytical lunatics bickering over the hot idea,
I'll not lack the head for a punctual nod-nod.
I'll nod to the professors' pontifications in the reapers' song—
Who dare discriminate in the feast of harvests?

Though I have not sown on the new Timescape,
I'll join the chorus in the reapers' song—
Who dare discriminate in the feast of harvests?

The Pauper

Richard Ntiru

Pauper, pauper, craning your eyes
In all directions, in no direction!
What brutal force, malignant element,
Dared to forge your piteous fate?
Was it worth the effort, the time?

You simply lean on a leafless tree
Nursing the jiggers that shrivel your bottom
Like a baby newly born to an old woman.
What crime, what treason did you commit
That you are thus condemned to human indifference?

And when you trudge on the horny pads,
Gullied like the soles of modern shoes,
Pads that even jiggers cannot conquer:
Does He admire your sense of endurance
Or turn his head away from your impudent presence?

You sit alone on hairless goatskins,
Your ribs and bones reflecting the light
That beautiful cars reflect on you,
Squashing lice between your nails
And cleaning your nails with dry saliva.

And when He looks at the grimy coating
Caking off your emaciated skin,
At the rust that uproots all your teeth
Like a pick on a stony piece of land,
Does He pat his paunch at the wonderful sight?

Pauper, pauper, crouching in beautiful verandas
Of beautiful cities and beautiful people,

Tourists and I will take your snapshots,
And your MP with a shining head and triple chin
Will mourn your fate in a supplementary question at Question
    Time.

How Can I Sing?   *Odia Ofeimun*

I cannot blind myself
to putrefying carcasses in the market place
pulling giant vultures
from the sky.

Nor to these flywhisks:
how can I escape these mind-ripping scorpion-tails
deployed in the dark
with ignominious licence
by those who should buttress faith
in living, faith in lamplights.

And how can I sing
when they stuff cobwebs in my mouth
spit the rheum of their blank sense
of direction in my eyes
—who will open the portals of
my hope in this desultory walk?

But I cannot blunt my feelers
to cheapen my ingrained sorrow
I cannot refuse to drink from
the gourd you hold to my lips

A garland of subversive litanies
should answer these morbid landscapes
my land, my woman.

Never Ask Me Why   *Odia Ofeimun*

My corpuscles don't readily
marry slogans.
Never ask me why

If you want to know
the sex of lagoons, jump
jump into their wombs

You will suffer
the swollen silence of rebirth

Never ask me why.
My country chews
the cud of civil strife

If you want to know
how my veins seethe
with the epithets being hurled
from the pith of this darkness
don't question your trigger, anymore
with that crooked finger.

You will suffer the swollen silence
of rebirth

(Don't question your trigger
anymore
with that crooked finger)

Or you'll be tearing the udders off
the lessons you should gain.

June 1969

Resolve . . .

To placate those the night surprised in their noons;
those we loaded with lead;
pushed to dungeons and makeshift graves;
to absolve our irretrievable selves
from the badger of willow-whips lurking in time.

We need no mourners in our stride,
no remorse, no tears.
Only this: Resolve
that the locust shall never again visit our farmsteads

Lenrie Peters

It is time for reckoning Africa
time for taking stock
never mind New York, America—
it's ours; is here, and running short

too long we have dragged
our slippered feet
through rank disorder
incompetence, self defeat

in the high capitals
the angry men; angry
with dust in their heads
a dagger at each other's throats

"Maudors" sit on wicker thrones
ghosted by White ants
a hundred Marabus at hand
living on the fat of the land

all threatening coups
and claiming vast receipts
like winsome children
feeding on mother's milk.

The seats of Government
levelled at the dice
they get the most
who tell the biggest lies

while honest men stand
waiting at the door
or rot in prison cells,
the vultures feed on sturgeon's eggs

The riot squads
parade the avenues
like lion prides
testing their sinews

and every trembling heart
retires as evening falls
crushed by the weight of hours
till daylight comes

oh country of great hopes
and boundless possibilities
will the seed grain
perish for ever

will rivers run
endlessly with blood,
saints resort to massacre
and all your harvests burn?

will no one see
no sign intruct
till Noah's ark
comes sailing on in flood?

between Alpha and Omega
is now; Africa
this is the lost time
and future time; Africa.

In this all revolutions end
and the straight path
from world to better world
branded across the sky.

Lenrie Peters

The sun has paled and turned away
    till after the Referendum

the moon holds portents great
    till after the Referendum

all fold their hearts and cross their breasts
    till after the Referendum

men scamper to a Lamprey's death
    after the Referendum

the morning glory blooms and blazes
    till after the Referendum

how about une nuit d'amour ma chère?
    After the Referendum!

Gulliver

Wole Soyinka

Once upon a ship-(of state)-wreck, where
The sun had shrunk the world at last to a true
Stature of deserving—the ant for unit—
I lay on earth tide-flung, obtruding

Miles of heart and mind, an alien hulk
Into a thumb assemblage. My feet
Were scaled as mountains. Fearful I was
Lest, rising, I dislodge a crossbeam
Of their skies. And this was well, I
Proved obedient to their laws: alien minds
Must learn recumbent postures. A brief
Impulse to unguided knowledge raised
A shower of needles, full-fanged, venom-bodied.
I took their meaning, pressed my hands
To earth. They quenched my fleshly thirst
In draughts of Lethe, and I was plunged
Deep in mindless trance. Wheels approached,
They bore me through the famished blades—
As dead the living come into necropolis—
Corded to a span of tumbrils, drugged.

They lodged me in a hall of sorts
A desecrated temple—and this proved sign
Of much that came to pass. I schooled me
In their ways, picked a wary course
Through egg-shell structures. I looked above
Their draughty towers, peered within
Secret chambers, and marvelled at their councils.
Peacock vain, mannikin cruel, sycophant.
The world was measured to a dwarf
Sufficiency; the sun by state decree
Was lowered to fit the sextant of their mind
And planets sighted lower to turn
In calculable grooves, in orbits centred
On the place of the Sun of suns,
Man-Mountain, King of Lilliput, Lord
And Terror of a thimble universe!

In such surrounds, in truth of fire
Was it a wonder I would sagely err?
How could a stranger tell an earthly sun
Identify as meteors matchwood tongues

Licking lawns, toy orchards, fairy groves?
In plainsight I decried an earthly burn
And squelched the puny flames in fountains
Of urine.
I sought nor favour nor reward, content
In civic duty done, presence of mind
Quick thinking. Alas! This act was rain
Upon long stunted passions,
Customs, taboos, parched sensibilities;
The storm unleashed within the chamberpot
Was long subsiding. Time passed. I kissed
The Queen's fingers. The land bestowed
A Royal Pardon. I pledged my strength anew
To service of the state, enticed the court
Statesmen, minions and nobility
To grace my temple home. They trod a measure
On the dais of my handkerchief
The king excelled in skating on a mucus
Rink—indeed we passed the rapid days
In feasts of love, in mirth and mutual service.

The seasons passed of peace, winds gathered
To a storm within an egg-cup.
Excavating scrolls in long forgotten archives
They stretched the warps of mind to rigid poles
Of opposition, blared the martial note:
From Us the Lillywhite King Lillypuss
To you obfuscating Blefuscoons
From Us the Herrenyolk of Egg
To you Albinos of the Albumen ... We Declare ...

I could not choose but serve
I took their measure in the depth
Of sea-beds, galley-slave to claims
Of bread and salt. I brought the enemy fleet
To port, and pressed a reasoned course
Of temperate victory. It did not suffice.
I pledged reversion of my strength

To arbitration; they pledged extinction of their kind.
At this rebellion of the galley-slave
They looked much, said little. I waded
Home in high-tide of their hate.

Indictments flowed at secret sessions
The palace deed re-echoes, concluding—
Imprimis: Unless by aid of Secret Powers
No human bladder could eject such potent
Piss to douse sidereal flames. Thus:
Imprimis: A blasphemer who dared mistake
Cosmic conflagration for mundane disaster, and—
For paradox: An arsonist for dwarfing
Flames of Lilliput with stark reflection.

From a capital doom, the saving thought
Was waste disposal—how rid the state
Of carrion weightier than the court and state.
The Court Hygienists voiced a dread
Of plagues, infections, cautioned—Hold!
A cult of septic hydrants may derive
From such a monumental corpse, springing
To douse orthodoxies of state and power
In rank corrosive draughts! A compromise
Was sought and found, the sentence writ:

The fault is not in ill-will but in seeing ill
The drab-horse labours best with blinkers
We pardon him to lose his sight to a cure
Of heated needles, that proven cure for all
Abnormalities of view—foresight, insight
Second sight and all solecisms of seeing—

Called vision.

The Analogy

Bahadur Tejani

Tonight
in the beggar
I saw the whole
of my country.

Tied were his hands—
ashamed of use—
for leprosy.

Sunk was his body
—eaten with corruption
—of the worm.

Like the
shattered snake
once liquid
now pounded
by innumerable feet
he dragged
himself
moisting the pavement
in the process.

What may I give?
A bullet in the brain
to end throes
infinitely greater
than death?

Or pity?

Is he cheating?

Lines for a Hindi Poet

Bahadur Tejani

Walking in the children's park
the poet said to me,
look: those dogs
playing at love

and these men
and their women
camera like
with photographic eyes
drinking deep at
founts of canine spontaneity.

"Verily," said the poet to me
"the brown man should learn
love from these dogs.
See how unafraid they are
how free."

I saw the bitch
offer her belly
but when he came
to smell her
she bounded like
a naughty child
and nipped him
with a quick-kissing mouth
and ran
so he should run after her.

And stood at bay.
defying him with the innocent passion
of a pure woman
with love in her eyes
necking gracefully when he came,
with an arched back

and free limbs
he rising and stooping
with her
in mock tension
of love-hostility.

I wanted to tear the sky
or rend the earth with my nails
shrieks to the wild wind
so a cataclysmic call would come.

Lord! Lord!
Let the brown blood
rediscover the animal
in itself,
and have free limbs
and laughing eyes of
love-play.
Lord, make these men
and their women
feel
that each to other
is not an untouchable.

The Silver Lining

Kalu Uka

We who walked through moon-flanked
    corridors of night
Have worshipped earnestly with gurgling reeds
    at interstices of rivers
We who stalked through agony-stitched
    brambles in our day
Have also seen bleared-eyed folk die
    when fireballs fall.

We have held on our tongues long parched
    rare nectar of other lands

We have strained through the sour vacuum
        where silence and neglect
Visited us. We have tarried patiently
        a cocoon fed on decaying tubers.

We who wore ash-bespattered bangles
        in meshes of our sorrow
We who dab on camwood, forsook incense
        to mourn disused blood
We women, ever girded round our tired loins
        with reams of peace,
We have also seen sucklings at our breast
        die without succour.

Then this morning a streak of light cut
Like a razor edge beside a new reed
Blooming on the top of the waters swept
By winds. A child saw, and cried out loud.

We too, long crusted and dormant like
The anger of Aetna lifted a face and saw
A broken cathedral spire rising again
As once it was, a towering hope, a sign
That all had not crashed to the basement.

VII
Cosmopolis

Song of Malaya   *Okot p'Bitek*

Sister Prostitutes
Wherever you are

I salute you

Wealth and Health
To us all

1 Karibu
Welcome ashore
You vigorous young sailor,
I see you scanning the horizon
In search of dry land

I hear your heart drumming
tum-tum-tu-tu-tum . . .

That time bomb
Pulsating in your loin
Surely weighs you down!
Oh . . . oh!

* * *

You soldier
Home bound,
I hear your song . . .
I see the girls
On the platform
Waving a farewell . . .

You reprieved murderer
You prisoner and detainee
About to be released,
Your granaries full
To overflow . . .

Welcome home!

* * *

You drunken Sikhs
The night club
Your battle ground,
Turbans, broken heads
And broken glass
Strewn on the floor ...

Are your wives here?

* * *

And you skinny
Indian vegetarian
Your wife breeding
Like a rat,
Welcome to my table too,
I have cooked red meat
With spices ...
You hairy
Thick-skinned white miner
At Kilembe, at Kitwe ...

You sweating engineer
Building roads and bridges,
I see the cloud of dust
Raised by your bumping Land Rover
Heading for the City.

Karibu, Come in,
Enter ...

* * *

All my thanks
To you
Schoolboy lover,
I charge you
No fee ...

That shy smile
On your face,
And . . .

Oh!
I feel ten years
Younger . . .

Hey! Listen . . .
Do not let the
Teacher know . . .
Mm . . . mmm?
He was there
Last night . . .!

*　*　*

Welcome you teachers
Teaching in bush schools,
I see you in buses
And on bicycles
Coming into the City
Your trouser pockets
Bulging with wallets . . .

Chieftain,
I see your gold watch
Glittering on your wrist,
You are holding
Your wife's waist
And kissing her
Goodbye.

Your shimmering briefcase
Is pregnant . . .

How long
Will your Conference last?
You bus drivers

and you taxi men
Driving away from your home towns,
Will you be back
Tonight?

* * *

You factory workers
Do you not hear
The bells?
Is that not the end
Of your shift?

You shop assistants
Standing there all day
Displaying your wares
And persuading the customers
With false smiles

When do you close?

* * *

Brother,
You leader of the People,
How is our Party doing?
How many rallies
Have you addressed today?
How many hands
Have you shaken?

Oh—oh . . .
Your blue shirt
Is dripping wet with sweat,
Your voice is hoarse,
You look a bit tired
Friend . . .

I have cold beer
In the house,
I have hot water
And cold water,
You must rest
A little,
Drink and eat
Something . . .

Brother,
Come!

* * *

Sister Harlots
Wherever you are,
Wake up
Wash up
Brighten up
Go gay and clean,
Lay
Your tables
Bring in fresh flowers . . .

Load your trays
With fresh fruits
Fresh vegetables
And plenty of fresh meat . . .
The hungry lions
Of the World
Are prowling around . . .
Hunting!

Ibadan   *J. P. Clark*

Ibadan,
        running splash of rust
and gold—flung and scattered
among seven hills like broken
china in the sun.

Mamana Saquina   *José Craveirinha*

Mamana Saquina
in the cosmopolitan, the dazzling mirage of the town
still kept her magic charms within her heart
at the hour of mourning
João.

Mamana Saquina
still kept the train's image in her mind
tangled with a song of steel on steel
to the beat João-Tavasse-went-to-the-mines
João-Tavasse-went-to-the-mines
João-Tavasse-went-to-the-mines
João-Tavasse-went-to-the-mines
João-Tavasse-went-to-the-mines

(On that morning of gilded cashew leaves
João Tavasse went to sign up at the depot)

And Mamana Saquina
stayed at Chibuto on the land
with Mamana Rosalina and cocuana Massingue
with ten hectares
in which to sow and bring to flower
the concession's seed

Night and day
the soul of Mamana Saquina swathed itself in nightmare
and buried itself in ten hectares of flowering cotton

(And João Tavasse
never came back to the depot)

Belching steam the miners' train pulled out
and in the pistons a voice sang
João-Tavasse-went-to-the-mines
João-Tavasse-went-to-the-mines
João-Tavasse-went-to-the-mines
João-Tavasse-went-to-the-mines

And Mamana Saquina mourned her son
scratched maize from the ground
and achieved the miracle of one hundred and fifty
five bales of cotton.

Abidjan

Ismael Hurreh

Abidjan, now is the time
when summer raindrops
hammer out

ringlets of memories
which hug the mutilated remains of Africa!

should Diop be resuscitated
should drums throb out rhythms of Rabearivelo
it is April, Abidjan
the time of summer raindrops.

Abidjan, these tortoise shells
which rattle through my voice
these are the lonely glass-maker's
whose bones sell millions of wraiths
that slave all clouded in dreams of tomorrow
who carves out images

of Africa's reunion
as time rolls into

ringlets of memories
and stirs dormant thoughts

now is the time
it is April, Abidjan
the time of summer raindrops.

O! Abidjan, these thorny words
thicker than thudding laughter

of diplomats
are these my golden thoughts

of you?
and the green oceans of eyes
my pride in the African forest
when are they going

to blossom at your doors?
and my Pan-African drums
have they all been

stolen at your doors?
should you have laughed at me
should you have smashed these drums

to pieces
it is April Abidjan

The Great Escapes   *Charles Kabuto Kabuye*

We're frightened men,
men without core or guts;
we move and act by group control;
we fear everything
with funny consequences.

our brand of religion is a chain of scapegods,
through it we fear to declare,
or discuss the movements of our humanity;
inside us our passions work
our emotions have ecstasies,
and our sentiments see truth:
all visions for our common survival.
but few of us will lift voice or finger
to acknowledge or utilize.
we escape even the best flower,
that fruit of our living flames of life,
hiding in the twilight inches of escapism:

> we never grow up to required maturity,
> for our eyes of depth and width,
> though active and sharp, never see,

or face the light: the epiphany of life and meaning embodied:

> we so hide from ourselves,
> remaining unmapped oases to ourselves.

and when we die,
the utility of our bodyself
faces the lie, the fear of our unexplored self
once so rich in gifts of joy and discovery:
yet all left with all energy and riches untouched.

Keep Off the Grass   *Oswald Mbuyiseni Mtshali*

The grass is a green mat
trimmed with gladioli
red like flames in a furnace.
The park bench, hallowed
holds the loiterer listening
to the chant of the fountain
showering holy water on a congregation
of pigeons.

KEEP OFF THE GRASS,
DOGS NOT UNDER LEASH FORBIDDEN.

Then madam walks her Pekinese,
bathed and powdered and perfumed.
He sniffs at the face of the "Keep Off" sign
with a nose as cold as frozen fish
and salutes it with a hind paw
leaving it weeping in anger and shame.

An Abandoned Bundle   *Oswald Mbuyiseni Mtshali*

The morning mist
and chimney smoke
of White City Jabavu
flowed thick yellow
as pus oozing
from a gigantic sore.

It smothered our little houses
like fish caught in a net.

Scavenging dogs
draped in red bandanas of blood
fought fiercely
for a squirming bundle.

I threw a brick;
they bared fangs
flicked velvet tongues of scarlet
and scurried away,
leaving a mutilated corpse—
an infant dumped on a rubbish heap—
"Oh! Baby in the Manger
sleep well
on human dung."

Its mother
had melted into the rays of the rising sun,
her face glittering with innocence
her heart as pure as untrampled dew.

African Poetry

Out on the horizon
there are fires
and the dark silhouettes of the beaters
with arms outstretched,
in the air, the green smell of burning palms.

African poetry

In the street

a line of Bailundu bearers
tremble under the weight of their load
in the room
a mulatto girl with meek eyes
colours her face with rice powder and rouge
a woman wriggles her hips under a garish cloth
on the bed
a man, sleepless, dreams
of buying knives and forks so he can eat at table
in the sky the glow
of fires

and the silhouette of black men dancing
with arms outstretched,
in the air, the hot music of marimbas

African poetry

and in the street the bearers
in the room the mulatto girl
on the bed the man, sleepless

The burnings consume
consume
the hot earth with horizons afire.

The Roses Are Withering

Richard Ntiru

The roses are withering
Our birth is only our death begun
Like tapers waste away the moment
They are lighted

"At the centre of every woman
Is a core of a prostitute."
So claimed Shannon of the Eunuchs' Order

Hasn't womankind resolved unanimously
That virginity is base selfishness
In the conduct of human relations
Their strong point is selfish generosity
Where is the eternal bonfire
But under the buttons of the jukebox
Where is your darling daughter
But at the bar counter
Perched with a fixed smile
Like a monkey on heat

Only the fat purses know the truth

The drought is imminent
The omen unmistakable
A crow makes holes in my roof
Mother-in-law strives to rival her daughter
Father angles for young blood in my wife

The Inspector keeps it up with a barmaid
At the corner in the bush in the Volvo
A dog and a bitch pass interlocked
They snarl and growl in approving recognition

The earth is baked
The seed dries and cracks under it
Fallen breasts are supported by textile props
Like ant-eaten walls

Oily shots with untucked shirts
Use their cheques as passport to sex
To recapture their youth on car cushions

The jackals move in the night with their sight
Birds keep in their nests and are they right

The headlines repeat the refrain
"Two bodies found in the river again
This time without a face
Crime strides at a sprightly pace"

Grandfather said
More in jest than in earnest
This is what he said
A senile dog's death
Begins by making it deaf
When men behave as manly men
A cow will give birth to a hen

The Bastard

B. S. Tibenderana

An unlucky creation,
His mother, a street walker;
His lying father,
A champion at producing bastards.

It's not his fault,
Poor innocent bastard,
That in slums he's brought up
By a mother that has no husband
Though many a husband he sees
Caressing his mother
On a stool or lumpy bed.

Poor bastard,
Dumped on the ground to make room
For his nocturnal fathers.

Or on the mat to spend his horrid nights
Among the steaming pots of food
And walking rats.

An unlucky creation,
This bastard,
Before birth heavily and mercilessly tormented
With a rope tied tight round the mother's waist
To strangle the foetus
Or his unformed head
Squeezed with hands rough and murderous.

Down latrines they are thrown,
These bastards,
For the ditch is the easiest way
And the mother's a girl again
Aye a virgin, and what a virgin!
Repaired and holy!
O crime! O murder of small flesh
That might have grown
To greatness and wisdom.

An unlucky creation,
This discharge of a street walker
All know his mother's a whore
His father a cheat;
Everyone knows
The bastard will beget bastards

Never will he know motherly love
Or feel soft hands,
Only the rough fist of old whores,
Dried breasts and stinking spittle,
And when his mother's gone
To earn her shilling
In the hot sun he will lie
In his own excrement
Under crows.

To bars they are brought,
The bastards
Thrown at the father
Like rotten pawpaws,
And he, to escape abuse and shame,
Runs faster than the kite,
His beer undrunk.

O Sanya Babies' Home know their secrets,
At her gate children mew like cats early in the morning
They are wrapped in sacks and rags
Their mother nowhere to be seen—
The child is gone, the load released,
Sanya Babies' Home will bear, of course, the cost.

Where could they get the money, the whores,
To feed the brats, when their own meal
Is a cassava stick with salt? Great drunkards
Who vomit on their knees in every bar
And drain old seed
from men they do not know.

VIII
Early Passage

To the Childless

You are the cold nests
In which the migrant bird lays no eggs
In which it never enters to brood;

You are the fruits that ripen, rot
And the wind blows you down
Dropping with a dead thud;
You are the ever cold hearths
In abandoned homesteads
In which the ghosts bathe the cold ashes
Your twin breasts
The two hearth stones that never support the Black Mother Pot.

Your wombs incommunicado with Earth
Shame, entombing an eternal void:
Mere beehives of drones
Encasements of belied watersheds—
Ever drying along the timescape
A spit into the angry bonfire;
You are the last breath that bubbled up God's throat.

And when the last breath is squeezed out of your chest;
And a needle is driven into the crust of your head
When your thumbs and last fingers
and tongue and testicles are mutilated
And a dead march escorts your coffin
And the last nail hammered into your tomb
Then know that
Your after-life rides on frothy crests of whirlwinds
Haunting only the insensible anthills.

The Spectacle of Youth

Mazisi Kunene

I loved the children of the lion
When their manes were beginning to grow,
Simulating the ancient heroes.
I knew the greatness of their future
When they leapt on the tender necks of antelopes
Which so long prided themselves on their fleetness
I praised the skilfulness of their power,
Knowing how soon they will be killing buffaloes.

Boy on a Swing

Oswald Mbuyiseni Mtshali

Slowly he moves
to and fro, to and fro,
then faster and faster
he swishes up and down.

His blue shirt
billows in the breeze
like a tattered kite.

The world whirls by:
east becomes west,
north turns to south;
the four cardinal points
meet in his head.

Mother!
Where did I come from?
When will I wear long trousers?
Why was my father jailed?

The Face of Hunger   *Oswald Mbuyiseni Mtshali*

I counted ribs on his concertina chest
bones protruding as if chiselled
by a sculptor's hand of famine.

He looked with glazed pupils
seeing only a bun on some sky-high shelf.

The skin was pale and taut
like a glove on a doctor's hand.

His tongue darted in and out
like a chameleon's
snatching a confetti of flies.

O! child,
your stomach is a den of lions
roaring day and night.

Lenrie Peters

Isatou died
When she was only five
And full of pride
Just before she knew
How small a loss
It brought to such a few.
Her mother wept
Half grateful
To be so early bereft.
And did not see the smile
As tender as the root
Of the emerging plant
Which sealed her eyes.
The neighbours wailed
As they were paid to do

And thought how big a spread
Might be her wedding too.
The father looked at her
Through marble eyes and said:
"Who spilt the perfume
Mixed with the morning dew?'

A Moment Already Gone

Isaac Rammopo

heaven draws curtains
gently aside
down the corridors of the mind

i knew not ˀ
till trembling transience had
breathed it away
i'd been
a watcher at the miracle of my own first perceiving;

had seen
through liquid layers
·down
to the white sands of the pool

where memory
of the long receding present

fades

and gropings now-wards
stumbles
along fresh untrodden byways
from the sanctum of nativity

it was a moment already gone
even as
i marvelled at the liquid radiance

in his eyes
and saw there the answer to
a question that
                but one quick breath ago
consumed the soul and died—
communed
with the sad irrecoverable aeons
of our days

I could have told him
without looking
but he was a child

I turned:
            there caught in the trellis of the bedroom window
            bleeding flames
            the cyclops eye of gold!
and he
on his knees
in his cot wonder-eyed
repeated: the sun, daddy?

Elegy of the Circumcized

L. S. Senghor

Night of childhood, blue Night, blond Night O Moon!
How often have I called to you, Night, crying by the roadside
By the side of the sorrows of my manhood? Solitude—and all
    about us are the dunes.
It was the night of earliest childhood, thick as pitch. Fear
    bowed our backs under the Lion's roaring.
Tall grasses bowed under the shifty silence of that night.
Fire of branches you fire of hope! Pale memory of the sun,
    heartening my innocence
Hardly at all. I had to die. I laid my hand on my throat like a
    girl who shudders at the horror of Death.
I had to die to the beauty of song—all things drift with the
    current of Death.

See the twilight on the throat of the dove when the blue
    pigeons call
And the seamews of dream fly with plaintive cries.

Let us die, let us dance, elbow to elbow woven together like a
    garland
No dress to hinder our steps, but the gift of the promise glows,
    lightning under the clouds.
Woi! the drum ploughs up the holy silence. Dance. Song lashes
    the blood
Rhythm drives out the fear that has us by the throat. Life
    holds death at bay.
Dance to the burthen of fear, that the night of the phallus may
    rise over our ignorance over our innocence.
Ah! die to childhood, let the poem die the syntax fall apart, let
    all the inessential words be swallowed up.
The weight of the rhythm is enough, no need of word-cement
    to build on the rock the City of tomorrow.
Let the sun rise from the sea of shadows
Blood! The waves are the colour of dawn.

But God, so many times I have wept—how many times?—for
    transparent nights of childhood.
Midday the Male is the hour of Spirits when every form strips
    off its flesh
Like the trees in Europe under the winter sun.
See, the bones are abstract, lending themselves only to
    calculations with straight edge, compass and sextant.
Life runs through the fingers of man like sand, crystals of snow
    imprison the life of the water
The serpent of water slips through the helpless hands of the
    reeds.
Dear Nights friendly Nights, Nights of Childhood, among the
    seaflats among the woods
Nights quivering with presences, brushed with eyelids, peopled
    with wings and sounds of breathing
And with breathing silence, say how many times have I
    sorrowed for you in the noontime of my age?

The poem droops in the sun of Noon, it feeds on the dew of
    evening
And the drum beats out the rhythm of the sap under the smell
    of ripened fruits,
Master of the Initiates, I know I need your wisdom to break
    the cipher of things
To learn my office as father, as lamarch
To measure exactly the field of my duties, to share out the
    harvest forgetting neither worker nor orphan.
The song is not only a charm, by it the woolly heads of my flock
    are fed.
The poem is bird-serpent, marriage of shadow and dawnlight
The Phoenix rises, he sings with wings extended, over the
    carnage of words.

Dedication
for Moremi, 1963   *Wole Soyinka*

Earth will not share the rafter's envy: dung floors
Break, not the gecko's slight skin, but its fall
Taste this soil for death and plumb her deep for life

As this yam, wholly earthed, yet a living tuber
To the warmth of waters, earthed as springs
As roots of baobab, as the hearth.

The air will not deny you. Like a top
Spin you on the navel of the storm, for the hoe
That roots the forests ploughs a path for squirrels.

Be ageless as dark peat, but only that rain's
Fingers, not the feet of men may wash you over.
Long wear the sun's shadow; run naked to the night.

Peppers green and red—child—your tongue arch
To scorpion tail, spit straight return to danger's threats
Yet coo with the brown pigeon, tendril dew between your lip

Shield you like the flesh of palms, skyward held
Cuspids in thorn nesting, insealed as the heart of kernel—
A woman's flesh is oil—child, palm oil on your tongue

Is suppleness to life, and wine of this gourd
From self-same timeless run of runnels as refill
Your podlings, child, weaned from yours we embrace

Earth's honeyed milk, wine of the only rib.
Now roll your tongue in honey till your cheeks are
Swarming honeycombs—your world needs sweetening, child.

Camwood round the heart, chalk for flight
Of blemish—see? it dawns!—antimony beneath
Armpits like a goddess, and leave this taste

Long on your lips, of salt, that you may seek
None from tears. This, rain-water, is the gift
of gods—drink of its purity, bear fruits in season.

Fruits then to your lips; haste to repay
The debt of birth. Yield man-tides like the sea
And ebbing, leave a meaning on the fossilled sands.

Incantation to Cause the Rebirth of a Dead Child
Traditional (from the Yoruba)

Death catches the hunter with pain.
Eshu catches the herbalist in a sack.
Shonponna is the snake that dies
And carries its children away.
Shonponna uses the invisible calabash
To kill two hundred people.
Eshu hands the invisible calabash to Shonponna.
The black soil of the earth is on the farm.

The red soil of heaven is in the grave.
You my child,
Oludande, you born-to-die,
Return from the red soil of heaven,
Come and eat the black soil of this world.

Ethics, Mores, Abstractions:
Man, the Philosopher

Trapped in a Puddle   *Amin Kassam*

how long will you fight
little ant
before you are crushed?
surviving rocks and
oppressive jungle
you felt invincible
strode on the sands
of the great lake
mocking the hissing waves,
yet you cling to a stone
in its chuckling belly
while they reach caressingly
for your soul—
not even the printed page
floating so invitingly
can save you from wrath.

Kindness   *Mazisi Kunene*

I waited for the restlessness
Of your hands
Holding all harvests of love.

At dawn
You walked in the wide fields of men
Who held you in their embrace.

You returned to the waiting crowds
Offering each one
His full vessel.

Triumph of Man

(on looking at sculpture)

Mazisi Kunene

At the sculptured face in the shadow of the stone
The angle turns with the vision of the flesh.
Even he who created from the essence lives.
He fought the claws of the eagle
Knowing how often it rose swollen with pride.
He overcame this moment of time
Making the silent speak.
The ages babble with the sound of eternity.
The dead awake and frolic in a dance.
Crushing the leaves that are daily scattered,
Because their faces have eyes,
And lips, and flesh, in the centuries.
The face that stands erect above the earth
Will turn its eyes, and plant its ears into time,
Listening to the rising epic of the years,
The years that boast with the ages of men
Who alone created eternity.

Time

Kojo Gyinaye Kyei

Time
   an accomplice of waste
               is an image of expense
it is always spilling
          its angry hands
                 wheeling
its consummate skill
          pounding
       like a drill on the brain
never to be stopped
          retrieved
        or
            replenished
forever whittling
         whittling

```
              whittling
          away
       away
     away
   away
 away
   all the vast stores
              of
                 being!
```

The Gourd of Friendship   *Richard Ntiru*

Where is the curiosity we've lost in discovery?
Where is the discovery we've lost in knowledge?
Where is the knowledge we've lost in communication?
Where is the communication we've lost in mass media?
Where is the message we've lost in the medium?
And where the community we've lost in all these?
It is easy to go to the moon:
There, there are no people.
It is easier to count the stars:
They will not complain.

' But the road to your neighbour's heart—
Who has surveyed it?
The formula to your brother's head—
Who has devised it?
The gourd that doesn't spill friendship—
In whose garden has it ever grown?
You never know despair
Until you've lost hope;
You never know your aspiration
Until you've seen others' disillusionment.
Peace resides in the hearts of men
Not in conference tables and delegates' signatures
True friendship never dies—
It grows stronger the more it is tested.

If It Is True

If it is true
that the world talks too much
then let's all keep quiet
and hear the eloquence
of silence

If it is true
that the world sees too much
then let's all close our eyes
and see the inner vision
beneath the closed eyes

If it is true
that the world hears too much
then let's wax our ears
and listen to the chastity of inner music
that defies betrayal
by the wayward wind

If it is true
that the world moves too much
then let's stand statuestill
and imitate the stubborn will
of trees
that move without being peripatetic

for the dumb don't tell lies

for the blind can't be peeping-toms

for the deaf cannot eavesdrop

for the crippled can't trespass.

Parachute men say
The first jump
Takes the breath away
Feet in the air disturb
Till you get used to it.

Solid ground
Is not where you left it
As you plunge down
Perhaps head first
As you listen to
Your arteries talking
You learn to sustain hope.

Suddenly you are only
Holding an umbrella
In a windy place
As the warm earth
Reaches out to you
Reassures you
The vibrating interim is over.

You try to land
Where green grass yields
And carry your pack
Across the fields

The violent arrival
Puts out the joints
Earth has nowhere to go
You are at the starting point

Jumping across worlds
In condensed time
After the awkward fall
We are always at the starting point

On Friendship and War

Roderic R. Roberts

Before the notorious storm takes heed
Of its intimate need—
To revenge quiet and peaceful mother earth,
A lot of things do happen, and of interest:
The clouds begin to shift mercilessly
And to change direction at random:
North, east; and rapidly, south-west—
All these actions,
With profound confusion and chaos.
The silvery butterflies
Are chased off the heavens,
And in their once glorified places,
Black robes lie down suspended—
Cold and wet.
Strong and fierce winds loaded to capacity
Gather motion on the season carpeted floor,
And a mixture of light and heavy rain
In rapid intermittent movements
Strikes at different parts
And with the ill notion of creating fear
To the occupants of mother earth:
Now here, now there;
Before assuming full control
Over the whole length.

The golden arrows of the fierce December days
Do not shine any more
With their respected brilliance;
When the collected forces of the storm
Rise up and are given the command
To attack,
Nothing is there that can stand within its path:
The crust of the earth erupts,
And human beings do nothing
But watch it destroy
And lay waste our efforts.

The relations of man to man differ little
To that of a storm:
Where friendship exists,
Our faces brighten up with smiles and joy,
And all the time
We wish another better health
Where friendship is a tribute to our souls,
Saline thoughts never gather themselves
Into mounds of height—
We develop toleration in our minds
As we struggle through the crisis of life
With nuclear warheads ticking on our backs.
And our ever functioning tongue
Take no leave
From producing honeyed language:
Praise slips unknowingly out of our parted lips,
And our experiences
Are shared with laughters and hand shakes.

But let friendship break to small bits,
And praise the common vulgar-hate:
Where close ties were once cherished,
Now this is a novelty,
If not a mid-afternoon dream:
It is only sad arrows which strike,
And they strike with strong force:
No more do lips part with an honest intent,
And a different tone is altogether noticed
Whenever encounters are honoured
With indifference—
(Being brought together by forces of circumstance.)
Therefore, where once
Eyes watered due to a stimulating sentence,
Now, those same eyes will open only a bit—
Two small horizons
Nursing dry patches of distaste.

The face will change its geography;
Ridges of varying number and size
Will suddenly be seen to exist—
(All these out of control,
Since man rarely tries to clear them:)
His system gets loose and out of function.
Just as the alliances between the land and the sea;
The heavens, the sea and the land break,
So is friendship, when hate takes full credit.

Freight Train
Tom Simpson

I've noticed you've been staring out the window for a long time—
Do you want to get off?
I've been travelling this train for twenty-three years,
Or so it seems;
Time becomes so distorted when you travel—
I may have just gotten on, that last stop.
You know, it seems all so inevitable for me,
This movement;
Many people aren't aware that they are actually here.

You say that you're afraid of getting off.
I guess that is what seems so inevitable to you . . .
Getting off.
You must fear the thought and the timefulness which follows.
Sit with me, would you?
Accept my hand,
Go with me and I will go with you.

Traditional (from the Swahili)

Give me the minstrel's seat that I may sit and ask you a word
my friends.
Let me ask for what reason or rhyme women refuse to marry:
Woman cannot exist except by man, what is there in that to
vex some of them so?

A woman is she who has a husband and she cannot but prosper.
Cleave unto your man and his kinsmen will become jealous.
His kinsmen have planted coco-palm, the teak, the mnga and
    the solanum tree.
When man goes on his road he goes with a friend, for he who
    walks alone has no good fortune
As man goes through life soon he is pierced by the thorn of
    misfortune
Or the sand-mote enters his eye and he needs a friend to
    remove it.
Even so do I advise you, the rich man and the poor man join
    hands across the shroud.
Better a loin-cloth without disgrace than a fine-flowered shawl
    of shame.

Cuckold Contented   *Traditional (from the Yoruba)*

My wife told me
I go to the market
I too went the market
Where I did not
Where I did not find my wife.
My friend told me
I go to my shop
I too went to the shop
Where I did not
Where I did not find my friend.
Walking on the beach
At the end of the day
I see the friend
Stretched out
On top of my wife.
With a thrust of my knife
I could have certainly
Certainly killed him
If he would not just in time
Just in time have awoken.

Just to give me
To give me five pounds
Five pounds which I took
And taking back with me
Taking back with me my wife.
Because water takes off the scent
The scent of love
And money doesn't smell
And money smells of nothing.

New Order

Kalu Uka

meteors draw to a close a certain fame
i draw a name to a certain close
nor downgrade the leprous scar
burning on each coffined soul.

but a coffin is limited, unlike
night where the soul never burns out
only retreats, recedes, recalesces
and soundings of its new tunes seep up.

i do not downgrade dark cavernous
wounds, or any wound, for the star
will repeat its fall, return to its sphere
though many weary years carry its light.

which is why i keep asking what night
is, what meteors choose day rather than
nightfall, what fame did not rise
by a fall, what triumph did not stand

by colossal failure in frail limited
woodwork such as is the casing earth
or the brittle, crumbled ancestor hearth
or the steel leprous technology of foreign

legions. meteors endure in time. night is time.
and here i draw to a close, rubbing
my scar, which is a cavernous wound,
the beginning and the end of fame and death.

X
Exile

Masked

Jared Angira

We left with the radiant rays
of the gleaming golden sun
and ascended the woody hills
past the thick green grazing lea

and volubly forded
the swift rolling river
that had bellied
humus and clay from the forested hills.

We heard wolves howl
on the massive rocks
and ferried the lake
with a deafening stony silence.
We came to the spacious arena
the wide field with myriad blossoms
each calling seductively for nectar
each calling cloying with beauty.

We opened our virgin palms
and received the potent juice from each
and they synthesized with
the beauty we had carried
and all of us went wild
with weighty rucksacks on our backs
and leather sandals
and we flew like balloons in frenzy.

Some broke their legs
Some broke their arms
Some went tipsy with nectar
and lost their way homewards.

Amid seismic snares I came home
and the black ram fled from me

because of my queer odour
which I brought from sojourn.

I knocked on my mother's reed door
and it smelled of burnt cowdung and goat's urine
she reluctantly opened
and showed me to sit on the kavirondo mat
that lay dusty and dry on the rugged floor.
I asked her to open the windows
There were NONE
I looked up and saw wasps and cobwebs
on the black roof

I went out to admire the meadow
and she slammed the reed door behind
and I went in my pedestal din
to the tingy locale from where I came.

Behind twanged the leather troubadour
and shone the black canopy
while ahead lay a giant fabric of smoke
and the only promise came
from the wide grassless navy blue sky.

Amagoduka at Glencoe Station   *Oswald Mbuyiseni Mtshali*

We travelled a long journey
through the wattle forests of Vryheid,
crossed the low-levelled Blood River
whose water flowed languidly
as if dispirited for the
shattered glory of my ancestors.

We passed the coalfields of Dundee—
blackheads in the wrinkled face
of Northern Zululand—
until our train ultimately came
to a hissing stop at Glencoe.

Many people got off
leaving the enraged train
to snort and charge at the night
on its way to Durban.

The time was 8 pm.

I picked up my suitcase,
sagging under the weight of a heavy overcoat
I shambled to the "non-European Males" waiting room.

The room was crowded
the air hung, a pall of choking odour,
rotten meat, tobacco and sour beer.

Windows were shut tight
against the sharp bite of winter.

Amagoduka* sat on bare floor
their faces sucking the warmth
of the coal fire crackling in the corner.

They chewed dried bread
scooped corned beef with rusty knives,
and drank *mqombothi* from the plastic can
which they passed from mouth to mouth.

They spoke animatedly
and laughed in thunderous peals.

A girl peeped through the door,
they shuddered at the sudden cold blast,
jumped up to fondle and leer at her
"*Hau! ngena Sisi!*—Oh! come in sister!"

She shied like a frightened filly
banged the door and bolted.

* Mine labour recruits.

They broke into a tumultuous laughter.

One of them picked up a guitar
plucked it with broken finger nails
caressed its strings with a castor oil bottle—

it sighed like a jilted girl.
"You play down! Phansi! Play D" he whispered.

Another joined in with a concertina,
its sound fluttered in flowery notes
like a butterfly picking pollen from flower to flower.

The two began to sing,
their voices crying for the mountains
and the hills of Msinga, stripped naked of
their green garment.

They crossed rivers and streams,
gouged dry by the sun rays,
where lowing cattle genuflected
for a blade of grass and a drop of water
on riverbeds littered with carcasses and bones.

They spoke of hollow-cheeked maidens
heaving drums of brackish water
from a far away fountain.

They told of big-bellied babies
sucking festering fingers
instead of their mothers' shrivelled breasts.

Two cockroaches
as big as my overcoat buttons
jived across the floor
snatched meat and bread crumbs
and scurried back to their hideout.

The whole group joined in unison:
curious eyes peered through frosted windows
"*Ekhaya bafowethu!*—Home brothers!"

We come from across the Tugela river,
we are going to EGoli! EGoli! EGoli!*
where they'll turn us into moles
that eat the gold dust
and spit out blood.

We'll live in compounds
where young men are pampered
into partners for older men.

We'll visit shebeens
where a whore waits for a fee
to leave your balls burning
with syphilitic fire.

If the gods are with us—
Oh! beloved black gods of our forefathers
What have we done to you
Why have you forsaken us—
We'll return home
to find our wives nursing babies—
unknown to us
but only to their mothers and loafers.

Waiting

Arthur Nortje

The isolation of exile is a gutted
warehouse at the back of pleasure streets:
the waterfront of limbo stretches panoramically—
night the beautifier lets the lights
dance across the wharf.
I peer through the skull's black windows

* Johannesburg.

wondering what can credibly save me.
The poem trails across the ruined wall
a solitary snail, or phosphorescently
swims into vision like a fish
through a hole in the mind's foundation, acute
as a glittering nerve.

Origins trouble the voyager much, those roots
that have sipped the waters of another continent.
Africa is gigantic, one cannot begin
to know even the strange behaviour furthest
south in my xenophobic department.
Come back, come back mayibuye
cried the breakers of stone and cried the crowds
cried Mr Kumalo before the withering fire
mayibuye Afrika

Now there is the loneliness of lost
beauties at Cabo de Esperancia, Table Mountain:
all the dead poets who sang of spring's
miraculous recrudescence in the sandscapes of Karoo
sang of thoughts that pierced like arrows, spoke
through the strangled throat of multi-humanity
bruised like a python in the maggot-fattening sun.

You with your face of pain, your touch of gaiety,
with eyes that could distil me any instant
have passed into some diary, some dead journal
now that the computer, the mechanical notion
obliterates sincerities.
The amplitude of sentiment has brought me no nearer
to anything affectionate,
new magnitude of thought has but betrayed
the lustre of your eyes.

You yourself have vacated the violent arena
for a northern life of semi-snow
under the Distant Early Warning System:

I suffer the radiation burns of silence.
It is not cosmic immensity or catastrophe
that terrifies me:
it is solitude that mutilates,
the night bulb that reveals ash on my sleeve.

Autopsy   *Arthur Nortje*

I

My teachers are dead men. I was too young
to grasp their anxieties, too nominal an exile
to mount such intensities of song;
knowing only the blond
colossus vomits its indigestible
black stepchildren like autotoxins.

Who can endure the succubus?
She who had taught them proudness of tongue
drank an aphrodisiac, then swallowed
a purgative to justify the wrong.
Her iron-fisted ogre of a son
straddled the drug-blurred townships,
breathing hygienic blasts of justice.

Rooted bacteria had their numbers
swiftly reduced in the harsh sunlight of arc-lamps,
the arid atmosphere where jackboots scrape
like crackling electric, and tape recorders
ingest forced words like white corpuscles,
until the sterile quarantine of dungeons
enveloped them with piteous oblivion.

In the towns I've acquired
arrive the broken guerrillas, gaunt and cautious,
exit visas in their rifled pockets
and no more making like Marx
for the British Museum in the nineteenth century,

damned: the dark princes, burnt and offered
to the four winds, to the salt-eyed seas. To their earth
unreturnable.

The world receives
them, Canada, England now that the laager
masters recline in a gold inertia
behind the arsenal of Sten guns. I
remember many, but especially one
almost poetic, so undeterrable.

II

He comes from knife-slashed landscapes:
I see him pounding in his youth across red sandfields
raising puffs of dust at his heels,
outclassing the geography of dongas
mapped by the ravenous thundery summers.
He glided down escarpments like the wind, until
pursued by banshee sirens
he made their wails the kernel of his eloquence,
turning for a time to irrigate
the stretches of our virgin minds.

Thus—sensitive precise
he stood with folded arms in a classroom
surveying a sea of galvanized roofs,
transfixed as a chessman, only
with deep inside his lyric brooding,
the flame-soft bitterness of love that recrudesces;
O fatal loveliness of the land
seduced the laager masters to disown us.

36,000 feet above the Atlantic
I heard an account of how they had shot
a running man in the stomach. But what is chilling
is how a warder kicked the stitches open
on a little-known island prison which used to be
a guano rock in a sea of diamond blue.

Over the phone in a London suburb he sounds
grave and patient—the years have stilled him:
the voice in a dawn of ash, moon-steady
is wary of sunshine which has always been
more diagnostic than remedial.

The early sharpness passed beyond to noon
that melted brightly into shards of dusk.
The luminous tongue in the black world
has infinite possibilities no longer.

Lenrie Peters

He walks alone
head bowed with memories
Exile in the park
some playful thing of long ago
glues him to a shop window

Faded suit sharp lined
loosely held by his proud heart
shoes scaled with polish
cannot comprehend; too much
to tell of harsh acceptances

No coward he
repository of rejected talents
an ounce of earth
silted weightily in his heart.
The breaking point is looking back

Crossed the Rubicon
race, nationality, ideology, religion
arrowed from earth to moon
founder of a new brotherhood
no hero he not of our nation born

Knows no tenderness
skin a mosaic of scars
heart in fixed deposit
safe from ridicule, decomposing
marionette-strings linked with stars

Exile go home
under your bed a bowl of tears
leave back streets
nightmare evenings kneeling in pews
brassy noises of homely fires

dream and wait.
Coarse cactus of desert wastes
perhaps tomorrow
sunflowers fading in the heat
will lie insensate at your feet.

Leaving the Country   *Bahadur Tejani*

Then the mind
became a body
immersed
in the water blanket of monsoon
a deep daze of dislocation
from colour
and creed
and country.

The vague ache
of memories
that interspersed
space time
like some lost children
in the forest
unworried by strange roads
because everything is unknown

unafraid of twilight
because all
is the long evening
wandering because
the unsure step onward
is the fate
function of limbs.

Yet terrified because
the forest is endless
and outside
through a pale patch
of the green darkness
the sun shines
like a chimera
that deepens the
global gloom.

Only one solace:
there have been
others too,
lingering in that twilight,
who shed
home and country·
and at times
colour
who travelled the long way
and also never felt happy.

A common hate enriched our love and us:

Escape to parasitic ease disgusts;
discreet expensive hushes stifled us
the plangent wines became acidulous

Rich foods knotted to revolting clots
of guilt and anger in our queasy guts
remembering the hungry comfortless.

In draughty angles of the concrete stairs
or seared by salt winds under brittle stars
we found a poignant edge to tenderness,

and, sharper than our strain, the passion
against our land's disfigurement and tension;
hate gouged out deeper levels for our passion—

a common hate enriched our love and us.

Dennis Brutus

The sounds begin again;
the siren in the night
the thunder at the door
the shriek of nerves in pain.

Then the keening crescendo
of faces split by pain
the wordless, endless wail
only the unfree know.

Importunate as rain
the wraiths exhale their woe
over the sirens, knuckles, boots;
my sounds begin again.

At a Funeral
Dennis Brutus

Black, green and gold at sunset: pageantry
And stubbled graves Expectant, of eternity,
In bride's-white, nun's white veils the nurses gush their bounty
Of red-wine cloaks, frothing the bugled dirging slopes
Salute! Then ponder all this hollow panoply
For one whose gifts the mud devours, with our hopes.

Oh all you frustrate ones, powers tombed in dirt,
Aborted, not by Death but carrion books of birth
Arise! The brassy shout of Freedom stirs our earth;
Not Death but death's-head tyranny scythes our ground
And plots our narrow cells of pain defeat and dearth:
Better that we should die, than that we should lie down.

(Velencia Majombozi, who died shortly after qualifying as a doctor)

Judgment of the Black Man
Kaoberdiano Dambara

The white man looked him in the face
my black brother did not stir

The white man shouted, roared, beat and kicked him
my black brother did not tremble

In his eyes there kindled flames
of rage, of dried tears, of force
My black brother did not stir, did not answer, did not tremble

In his steady eyes there kindled the flame
of a force which only the black man knows.

João was young like us
João had wideawake eyes
and alert ears
hands reaching forwards
a mind cast for tomorrow
a mouth to cry an eternal "no"
João was young like us

João enjoyed art and literature
enjoyed poetry and Jorge Amado
enjoyed books of meat and soul
which breathe life, struggle, sweat and hope
João dreamt of Zambezi's flowing books spreading culture
for mankind, for the young, our brothers
João fought that books might be for all
João loved literature
João was young like us

João was the father, the mother, the brother of multitudes
João was the blood and the sweat of multitudes
and suffered and was happy like the multitudes
He smiled that same tired smile of shop girls leaving work
he suffered with the passivity of the peasant women
he felt the sun piercing like a thorn in the Arabs' midday
he bargained on bazaar benches with the Chinese
he sold tired green vegetables with the Asian traders
he howled spirituals from Harlem with Marion Anderson
he swayed to the Chope marimbas on a Sunday
he cried out with the rebels their cry of blood
he was happy in the caress of the manioc-white moon
he sang with the shibalos their songs of homesick longing
and he hoped with the same intensity of all
for dazzling dawns with open mouths
to sing
João was the blood and sweat of multitudes
João was young like us.

João and Mozambique were intermingled
João would not have been João without Mozambique
João was like a palm tree, a coconut palm
a piece of rock, a Lake Niassa, a mountain
an Incomati, a forest, a maçala tree
a beach, a Maputo, an Indian Ocean
João was an integral and deep rooted part of Mozambique
João was young like us.

João longed to live and longed to conquer life
that is why he loathed prisons, cages, bars
and loathed the men who make them.
For João was free
João was an eagle born to fly
João loathed prisons and the men who make them
João was young like us.

And because João was young like us
and had wideawake eyes
and enjoyed art and poetry and Jorge Amado
and was the blood and sweat of multitudes
and was intermingled with Mozambique
and was an eagle born to fly
and hated prisons and the men who make them
Ah, because of all this we have lost João
We have lost João.

Ah, this is why we have lost João
why we weep night and day for João
for Joao whom they have stolen from us.

And we ask
But why have they taken João,
João who was young and ardent like us
João who thirsted for life
João who was brother to us all
why have they stolen from us João
who spoke of hope and dawning days

João whose glance was like a brother's hug
João who always had somewhere for one of us to stay
João who was our mother and our father
João who would have been our saviour
João whom we loved and love
João who belongs so surely to us
oh why have they stolen João from us?
and no one answers
indifferent, no one answers.

But we know
why they took João from us
João, so truly our brother.

But what does it matter?
They think they have stolen him but João is here with us
is here in others who will come
in others who have come.
For João is not alone
João is a multitude
João is the blood and the sweat of multitudes
and João, in being João, is also Joaquim, José
Abdullah, Fang, Mussumbuluco, is Mascarenhas
Omar, Yutang, Fabiao
João is the multitude, the blood and sweat of multitudes

And who will take José, Joaquim, Abdullah
Fang, Mussumbuluco, Mascarenhas, Omar, Fabiao?
Who?
Who will take us all and lock us in a cage?
Ah, they have stolen João from us
But João is us all.
Because of this João hasn't left us
and João "was" not, be "is" and "will be".
For João is us all, we are a multitude
and the multitude
who can take the multitude and lock it in a cage?

Heroic Shields

Mbella Sonne Dipoko

The sun is rising.
In their nakedness the karoos will all be hot again
But you will shiver in spite of it
In the memory of trekkers who left you there
To be feverish in the shadows of days of doubt
And the nightmare of Great Chaka
Still alive in your eternal Zulu dream.

Last night, anguished tyrant
You dreamt of the hero whose people you fear
And of the charging of heroic shields
Today you tremble, Voortrekker, staring at the Vaal
And the diamonds of your heart.

Fear Shall Fail

Tsegaye Gabre-Medhin

Yet fear shall fail to conquer our warmth
Since each has
A sunny side of a cause to serve,
Though distant cries come breaking
On our threshold
And homes tremble
With the terror of the earth,
Though glories are uprooted
And many more shall be.
Though heroes lament
Birds wail
Fowls feast
And waterfalls sucked dry
Yet fear shall fail to conquer our warmth.

Yet fear shall fail to conquer our warmth
Since each has
A god of love to worship,
Though our daily tasks
Amount to serving in a tag of war

As aimless dummies
Or stumbling blocks for one another
By the dry motor of convenience
That cuts us into passable shapes,
Though our dreams prevalently holds
Of machine monsters and clock masters.
Our off-the-shoulder wisdoms boil
Into mere forget-me-nots
And our energies for better intentions
Consumed in a naked battle of wits
Yet fear shall fail to conquer our warmth.

Yet fear shall fail to conquer our warmth
Since each has
A dream to out-dream others,
Though flowers cease to charm us
And man seems
In the asylum of a beatnik-bomb-age
Or hand on
In a chino-american wrestle world,
Though men forget to sing
And their senses tuned
To the crash of cymbals,
Wombs cease to fertilize
And in place of breasts
False teeth grown,
Though time is devoid of human bondage
And each dies a death of his own
Yet fear shall fail to conquer our warmth.

Those Strange Times

Armando Guebuza

Those strange times
Which smothered in sweat
The day's full length
And peopled the fearful night
With shadows
Of a new day

Those strange times
Which stormed existence
And eroded
The hopes for a new lif e
Leaving behind
The blackness of anguish

Those strange time
Which shrouded the Mother Earth
Killing hope
And sowing despair

Those strange times
When the whip hissed
And tore
A man's living flesh
Raising a cry of rage
- inert rage

Those strange times
When the affront
Blew burning
Through the cells of a brain rebelling at humiliation
And remained ... Inert

Those strange times
Times of dense shadows
Times of anguish
Times of humiliation
Times of inert rage
Those times have vanished defeated

This is a time of the certainty of a joyful day
This is a time of war against rottennes
This is time of revolt against the whid
This is the time of armed struggle .

Sitting on a stool outside his mud hut,
The mzee scratched his head in a slow motion,
Trying to recall.
His dim grey eyes quiveringly stared into the distance
And with a faint faltering voice he spoke
Of the wind that stirred sinister feelings,
Of the leaves that rustled with foreboding,
Of the men who talked of deliverance and freedom,
And of the warriors who pledged to fight.
Then he paused and snuffed some tobacco
"The Germans—" He shook his head and shuddered:
"Yes, they came—with guns, to be sure—
Many guns."
His glance slowly shifted in a broken semi-circle
At each of the few listeners who squatted on the ground.
He pointed to the distant hills on his right:
"For many days,
They resounded with drum-beats and frenzied cries;
Then with the spirits of alien ancestors
They thundered with strange unearthly sounds."
Placing both his hands on his head,
He looked down on the earth and pronounced,
"They fired bullets, not water, no, not water."
He looked up, with a face crumpled with agony,
And with an unsteady swing of his arm, he said,
"Dead, we all lay dead."
While the mzee paused, still and silent,
His listeners gravely looked at each other
Seeming to echo his last words in chorus.
Finally, exhausted, he sighed,
"The Germans came and went,
And for many long years
No drums beat again."

Mandela's Sermon

Blessed are the dehumanized
For they have nothing to lose
But their patience.

False gods killed the poet in me. Now
I dig graves
With artistic precision.

Point of Departure: Fire Dance Fire Song *Keorapetse Kgositsile*

*(A wise old man told me in Alabama: "Yeah, Ah believes in nonviolence
alright. But de only way to stay nonviolen' in dis man's country is to keep a
gun an' use it." Four years earlier another wise old man had told me the same
thing near Pietersburg in South Africa. He said his words of wisdom in
Sepedi.)*

I The Elegance of Memory

Distances separate bodies not people. Ask
Those who have known sadness or joy
The bone of feeling is pried open
By a song, the elegance
Of colour a familiar smell, this
Flower or the approach of an evening . . .

All this is NOW

I used to wonder
Was her grave warm enough,
'Madikeledi, my grandmother,
As big-spirited as she was big-legged,
She would talk to me. She would . . .
How could I know her sadness then
Or who broke my father's back?
But now . . .

The elegance of memory,
Deeper than the grave
Where she went before I could
Know her sadness, is larger
Than the distance between
My country and I. Things more solid
Than the rocks with which those sinister
Thieves tried to break our back

I hear her now. And I wonder
Now does she know the strength of the fabric
She wove in my heart for us? . . . Her
Voice clearer now than then: Boykie,
Don't ever take any nonsense from them,
You hear!

           There are memories between us
Deeper than grief. There are
Feelings between us much stronger
Than the cold enemy machine that breaks
The back. Sister, there are places between us
Deeper than the ocean, no distances.
Pry your heart open, brother, mine too,
Learn to love the clear voice
The music in the memory pried
Open to the bone of feeling, no distances

II Lumumba Section

Searching past what we see and hear
Seeing past the pretensions of knowledge
We move to the meeting-place,
The pulse of the beginning the end and the beginning
In the stillnesses of the night
We see the gaping wounds where
Those murderers butchered your flesh
As they butchered the flesh of our land
Spirit to spirit we hear you
Then blood on blood comes the pledge

Swift as image, in spirit and blood
The sons and daughters of our beginnings
Boldly move to post-white fearlessness
Their sharpnesses at the murderer's throat
Carving your song on the face of the earth
In the stillnesses of the night
Informed by the rhythm of your spirit
We hear the song of warriors
And rejoice to find fire in our hands
"Aint no mountain high enough . . ." Dig it,
The silences of the wind know it too
"Aint no valley low enough . . ."
Freedom, how do you do!

III Fire Dance

There will be no dreaming about escape
There will be no bullshit coldwar talk
        The fire burns to re-create
        the rhythms of our timeless acts
        This fire burns timeless in our
        time to destroy all nigger chains
        as real men and women emerge
        from the ruins of the rape of white greed

        The rape by savages who want to control
        us, memory, nature. Savages who even forge
        measures to try to control time. Don't you
        know time is not a succession of hours!
        Time is always NOW, don't you know!
        Listen to the drums. That there is a point of departure
        NOW is always the time. Praise be to Charlie Parker
        And it don't have nothing to do with hours

Now sing a song of NOW
A song of the union of pastandfuture
Sing a song of blood—The African miner, his body
Clattering to the ground with mine phthisis:
That there is murder. Do the dance of fire

The rhythm of young black men
Burning these evil white maniacs
Their greedy hands clattering to the ground
Like all their vile creations

Do our thing for the world, our world
NOW's the time, NOW's the time
A breath of love, song for my woman
Fire in her breast for our children
Supreme as a climax with the music of the wind
In her divine thigh there is life there is fire

The Screams

Mazisi Kunene

I offer you screams of a thousand mad men
Who scream to those without mercy
Who scream over the graveyards
Of skeletons, piled on piles,
Bones dislocated from their joints.

I offer you voices of a thousand vultures
Who hover over fields of flesh
Where columns abandon columns in the hill
Where the eyes are lost in the sockets
Where the moon abandons them in the wilderness.

I offer you the cloth that is torn in the middle
Left in the field
By those who departed before the children were weaned from
    the breast
Tell me, tell me,
Who wore it before the fall of winter?

I offer you those who sleep alone
With their hands folding the dream,
A dream that will never come
Because they stare in the night of death,
I offer them to you to shout them to the world!

Tribute to Joan Baez on Vietnam

Mazisi Kunene

Mshengu, mother of dawn,
You who traversed the hills of the Ethiopians
And returned with a dream,
Spread your wings over the girl's stone
And sing a great song at the waterfalls;
Feed it with the gourds of your breasts
When they burst above the day,
May they be the heritage of the generation of Nkulu
Because you alone, whose heart is vast,
You distributed hearts from the islands.

Thought on June 26

Mazisi Kunene

Was I wrong when I thought
All shall be avenged?
Was I wrong when I thought
The rope of iron holding the neck of young bulls
Shall be avenged?
Was I wrong
When I thought the orphans of sulphur
Shall rise from the ocean?
Was I depraved when I thought there need not be love,
There need not be forgiveness, there need not be progress,
There need not be goodness on the earth,
There need not be towns of skeletons,
Sending messages of elephants to the moon?
Was I wrong to laugh asphyxiated ecstasy
When the sea rose like quicklime
When the ashes on ashes were blown by the wind
When the infant sword was left alone on the hill top?
Was I wrong to erect monuments of blood?
Was I wrong to avenge the pillage of Caesar?
Was I wrong? Was I wrong?
Was I wrong to ignite the earth

Watching Europe burn with its civilization of fire,
Watching America disintegrate with its gods of steel,
Watching the persecutors of mankind turn into dust
Was I wrong? Was I wrong?

The Master of the House

Oswald Mbuyiseni Mtshali

Master, I am a stranger to you,
but will you hear my confession?

I am a faceless man
who lives in the backyard
of your house.

I share your table
so heavily heaped with
bread, meat and fruit
it huffs like a horse
drawing a coal cart.

As the rich man's to Lazarus,
the crumbs are swept to my lap
by my Lizzie:
"Sweetie! eat and be satisfied now,
Tomorrow we shall be gone."

So nightly I run the gauntlet,
wrestle with your mastiff, Caesar,
for the bone pregnant with meat
and wash it down with Pussy's milk.

I am the nocturnal animal
that steals through the fenced lair
to meet my mate,
and flees at the break of dawn
before the hunter and the hounds
run me to ground.

The Washerwoman's Prayer
to my mother-in-law

Oswald Mbuyiseni Mtshali

Look at her hands
Raw, knobbly and calloused.
Look at her face
Like a bean skin soaked in brine.

For countless years she has toiled
To wash her master's clothes
Soiled by a lord's luxuries.

In frost-freckled mornings,
In sun-scorched afternoons,
She has drudged murmurless.

One day she fell and fainted
With weariness.
Her mouth a foaming spout
Gushing a gibberish.

"Good Lord! Dear Lord!" she shouted
"Why am I so tormented?
How long have I lamented?.
Tell me Lord, tell me O Lord."

"My child! Dear child," she heard
"Suffer for those who live in gilded sin,
Toil for those who swim in a bowl of pink gin."

"Thank you Lord! Thank you Lord.
Never again will I ask
Why must I carry this task."

Western Civilization

Agostinho Neto

Sheets of tin nailed to posts
driven in the ground
make up the house.

Some rags complete
the intimate landscape.

The sun slanting through cracks
welcomes the owner

After twelve hours of slave
labour.

breaking rock
shifting rock
breaking rock
shifting rock
fair weather
wet weather
breaking rock
shifting rock

Old age comes early

a mat on dark nights
is enough when he dies
gratefully
of hunger.

Requiem for the Saboteurs

Isaac Rammopo

I This Night
Out here in the night
the keen edge of Winter
cuts, raw; grit stings,

flung from the brooding
brows of tow'ring
sandy-headed gods,
out here in the night.

Chained all through the night,
the saxophone wails
trumpet whines
trombone murmurs,
pleading transition into happier mood
night after night
after night
and no kindly hand
no feather touch to move
the stylus into gayer groove,
end the agony,
stay the blight.

Out here this night
warm bones twirl in fitful delirium
churned in the maelstrom of muted saxophones,
trumpets whining
trombones murmuring,
this final fling,
out here this night;
for this night
at midnight
the drum's uneasy rumble breaks out in wild unrhythmic tattoo;
flesh fried
pungent with dash of powder
marrow for measure
reeking in Heaven's tardy nostrils,
sharp cry
pinned under brick and mortar
shrapnel-sharpened,
back-bone broken
dead limbs cragged on purple ribbons
into the night.

This night
the moaning saxophone shall cease
her melancholy piece,
and the bitter cold of Winter nights
mellow in the warmth of Summer days.

Capital

Wole Soyinka

It cannot be
That germ which earth has nurtured
Man tended—once I watched a waterfall
Of germ, a grain-spray plenitude
Belched from chutes of wide-mouthed
Glad satiation; I swear the grains
Were singing—

It cannot be
That policy, deliberation
Turns these embers of my life
To ashes, and in polluted seas
Lays sad beds of yeast to raise
Dough
On the world market.

The White Pumpkin

Enoch Tindimwebwa

His gun on his shoulder,
A hat pulled like a basin over his head,
The white pumpkin came over the hill.
His shorts looked like a woman's skin skirt
His gun like a baking stick
He resembled and was taken for
A Woman.

Crying in terror
The naked children fled
Followed by their mothers
With babies dangling on their backs.

"An evil white spirit!" men cried,
"A white monster!"
And within the wink of an eye
The village was empty.

Far away they fled
Into the deep forest's breast
Among mosquitoes and potholes of elephant.

Expecting a roll of drums
The white pumpkin wondered
At finding the village so empty and still.
Then stooping like a marabou, long-nosed,
He went into a hut,
O horror! O foul stench
Of rotting turds!

He stood there amazed and fascinated.
This was revelation. This was discovery.
This was the true heart of Africa . . .
A fire, compact and living
That licked three spherical stones
On top a fat pot
Simmering and spitting.

In the hut's shadow
A huge wooden bed.
Behind it, goats,
The black pot coughed and belched
With its load of beans,
In the roof, rats wrestled.

He stood there
His breast thumping
Unwelcomed,
And furiously he cried:
"Where have these savage bastards gone,"

Then from a small rectangular box
He drew a flame
And set the village, the whole village afire.

I saw it. I saw it all
And I saw him wash himself
Behind a grain-bin.
I saw his chest
That was hairy as a dog's, and pumpkin white.

Tchicaya U Tam'si

As best he can each dies alone,
I will curl up in the crater
of a vapourish volcano
or else flush myself away
down the rung changes of the road
And if till the road's end
my heart can hold out
I do not see why
my blood should not swirl
under the arch uprooting
from the flood of my human past,
from my agony-given face, ·
the sign of the cross or the harbour
where we set sail
in quest of a common belly
to save us from a common grave!

Better drown me in blood
than in the fires of the bush!

Everywhere the deer dissolve
the fires already in their eyes;
And a randy death they die.

Stressing the *i* in cries or crime
until dead drunk,
and the bugles blow you awake
and drag you into the ring alone.

Kitona or Kamina
Congolese!
Blood blood blood
rolling to the funeral drums
The moon shakes out the shroud;
the muezzin no longer copes
still worse after his death compassed
with a schoolboy's application
rounding the o in omega
or the eyes in astonishment!

His last stagger executes
the steps of the twist
and when he softly drops
the cause is his randy death

As best he can each dies alone . . .

Fragile   *Tchicaya U Tam'si*

> The night roars on
> one dies of love for the stars
> it is only a sinful swan
> Certain great ideas
> now obsolete
> the night roars on

Everything different!

A dance of hour-glass eyes
filtered to measure the age of a child
shaped for the life which flees from death!

What choreographer is mad enough
for this cold art
this drifting of five continents

Pith of shadow, has it, like my sense
the dorsal fin of the algae
to hold it upright in the sun

Endlessly I decalcify my joy
and lo its hands become islands
they surpass the Antilles!
Child I cling no longer to the Zaïre
I am no more master of my tears
master of this patchwork of time

what flowers to dress
for Emmett Till
child whose soul is bleeding in my own!

They killed him under the water
His mother threw his arms in the fire
to cook her midday meal
At once the sun miserable riot
of eunuch Caciques
smashed itself to pieces in his childish eyes
at his first ecstasy!
Then the strange martyrology—Mother
I knew it!
The memory of that flesh burns deeper
than this sudden fire which seizes the arms
for his meal neither of noon or evening
He that death dissects with a flurry of kicks
in the loins ... the story goes that the child greeted a wanton
woman in the crowd ... that evening he went to the shore
to watch the tide of the river ... he wanted to sing the soul
of that wanton woman ... he had greeted: they killed him
     under water

as they baptize hereabouts
in such christian fashion
never with a mother's name!

We were men of night
A return of the tidal wave would have saved all
but am I the sponsor of storms?
They had not stripped my tree.

I condemn myself to live on my tomorrows
without singing of my leaves.
I die of the delirium of ecstasy
The world which poisons me
leaves me more memories than the nightingale has scales to sing
in his dawn sadness

And then the sea at noon
waveless, hoisting its ships ashore
Is that their crime?

I die alone from pride
I leave to Emmett Till his death
from horror of myself

Who loves the sun enough to throw
body and soul there?

I also have known the sun at noon
without the softness of water
on a sea without waves or ships
at large upon a crowded beach!

And now the plain where I live
my hand rests heavy on my door
take my share of fruits
though I know not from what tree they come
take my share of tears

even though I know what heart they waste
Be quick
I am already far from my source

Be quick
I can be useful
I have already trimmed my nails
shaved my head
I stand clean before the night

XII
Land and Liberty

There are on the earth 50,000 dead whom no one
    mourned
        on the earth
            unburied
                50,000 dead
whom no one mourned

A thousand Guernicas and the message in the
    brush-strokes of Orozco and
            de Siqueiros

it had the dimensions of the sea, this silence
spread across the land

        as if the rains rained blood
        as if the coarse hair was grass many metres high
        as if the mouths condemned
        in the very moment of their 50,000 deaths
        all the living of the earth

There are on the earth 50,000 dead
whom no one mourned

no one . . .

the mothers of Angola
        died together with their sons.

Here We Were Born

I

The land where we were born
goes back
like time

Our forefathers
were born
and lived
in that land

and they, like the coarse wild grass
were the meagre body's veins
running red, earth's fragrance.

Trees and granite pinnacles

their arms
embraced the earth
in daily work
and sculpting the new world's fertile rocks
began, in colour,
the great design of life.

II

And it was also
here
that you and I were born

Hot land
of rising sun

Green land
of fertile fields

Soft land
with a broad bosom

It was to us
all this surrendered
brimming with life
and amorous longing.

III

We grew up lulled
by the Chirico's song
and as we reached in this way the level of Man
the impetus was such it generated
waves pregnant with crystal.

And when the wind
whips the sky
and the sword falls
tearing flesh

and horror touches
the naked face

Our love is not shaken

This is the land
where we were born

its sorrow
is our grief

and today's bitter cloud
is a moment's pain
which the rain must dry.

IV

Our land is open
to the frank embrace of hope

In the wake of past steps
free orbs come shining

and, as a young brother
of an old land
let us go
lifting in broad hands
our fathers' heritage
and with the leaves of the heart
carry on man's work
the great design of life.

Love Poem

Antonio Jacint

*También como la tierra
yo pertenezco a todos.
No hay una sola gota
de odio em mi pecho. Abiertas
van mis manos
Esparciendo las uvas
en el viento*

Pablo Neruda

*(Like the earth, I belong to
everyone. There is not a single
drop of hatred in my breast.
Open wide, my hands scatter grapes
in the wind.)*

When I return to see the sun's light they deny me
my love
we shall go dressed in peace
and wearing a smile of flowers and fruit
entwined
along roads—twisting snakes
among the coffee groves
climbing from the mountains to the stars
and to our shining dreams
we shall go
singing the songs that we know and do not know

When I return to see the sun's light they deny me
my love
we shall go

then go briefly to weep
on the countless graves of countless men
who have gone
without funeral or wake
without hope for the sun's light they deny us

We shall go, my love
and tell them
I have returned, we are returning
because we love each other
and we love
those countless graves of countless men

When I return to see the sun's light they deny me
with standards raised
—freedom is a fruit of harvest—
we shall go
and gather corn cobs and colours
and offer flowers and resurrection to the dead
and to the living, the strength of our own lives
my love
we shall go
and draw a rainbow on the paper sky
for our son to play with:

> rain may come and rain may go
> if Our Lady wills it so
> rain for the father's farm will run
> and never, never send for the sun

We shall go, my love, we shall go
when I return
—the bars undone—
and embraced together we'll make
life, undeniable, continue
in the gentle gifts of harvest
in the chirping of startled birds
in the march of men returning

in the rains' hosannas on the reborn earth
in the confident steps of a people resolved
my love.

A fringe of new colour will dress the earth
we shall make kisses and smiles the tissue of life
and between the endless cotton fields
and the dances of a joyful feast

we shall go
my love.

Agostinho Neto

February*

It was then the Atlantic
in the course of time
gave back the carcasses of men
swathed in white flowers of foam
and in the victims' boundless hate,
brought on waves of death's congealed blood

And the beaches were smothered by crows and
jackals with a bestial hunger for the battered flesh
on the sands
of the land, scorched by the terror of centuries
enslaved and chained,
of the land called green
which children even now call green for hope.

It was then that the bodies in the sea
swelled up with shame and salt
in the course of time
in blood-stained waters
of desire and weakness.

* The Angolan revolution began on 4 February 1961 with an attack

ıt was then that in our eyes, fired
now with blood, now with life, now with death,
we buried our dead victoriously
and on the graves made recognition
of the reason men were sacrificed
for love,
for peace,
even while facing death, in the course of time,
in blood-stained waters

And within us
the green land of San Tome
will be also the island of love.

Hoisting the Flag

Agostinho Neto

When I returned
the soldier ants had vanished from the town
And you too
My friend Liceu
voice gladdening with hot rhythms of the land
through nights of never-failing Saturdays,
You too
sacred and ancestral music
resurgent in the sacred sway of the Ngola's rhythm,
You too had vanished
and with you
the intellectuals
the Ligue
Farolim
the Ingombata meetings
the conscience of traitors betraying without love.
I came just at the moment of the dawning cataclysn.
as the seedling bursts the rain damped ground
thrusting up resplendent in youth and colour,
I came to see the resurrection of the seed,
the dynamic symphony of joy growing among men.

And the blood and the suffering
was a tempestuous flood which split the town.

When I came back
the day had been chosen
and the hour was at hand.

Even the children's laughter had gone
and you too
my good friends, my brothers,
Benge, Joaquim, Gaspar, Ilidio, Manuel
and who else?
hundreds, thousands of you, my friends,
some for ever vanished,
ever victorious in their death for life.

When I came back
some momentous thing was moving in the land
the granary guards kept closer watch,
the school children studied harder
the sun shone brighter,
there was a youthful calm among the old people,
more than hope—it was certainty
more than goodness—it was love.

Men's strength
soldiers' courage
poets' cries
were all trying to raise up
beyond the memory of heroes.
Ngola Kiluanji,
Rainha Jinga,
trying to raise up high
the flag of independence.

Poem

Come, brother and tell me your life
come, show me the marks of revolt
    which th· enemy left on your body

Come, say to me "Here
my hands have been crushed
because they defended
the land which they own

"Here my body was tortured
because it refused to bend
to invaders

"Here my mouth was wounded
because it dared to sing
my people's freedom"

Come brother and tell me your life,
come relate me the dreams of revolt
which you and your fathers and forefathers
dreamed
in silence
through shadowless nights made for love

Come tell me these dreams become
war,
the birth of heroes,
land reconquered,
mothers who, fearless,
send their sons to fight.

Come, tell me all this, my brother.

And later I will forge simple words
which even the children can understand
words which will enter every house

like the wind
and fall like red hot embers
on our people's souls.

In our land
Bullets are beginning to flower.

A Different Poem
Onésimo Silveira

The people of the islands want a different poem
For the people of the islands;
A poem without exiles complaining
In the calm of their existence;
A poem without children nourished
On the black milk of aborted time
A poem without mothers gazing
At the vision of their sons, motherless.
The people of the islands want a different poem
For the people of the islands:
A poem without arms in need of work
Nor mouths in need of bread
A poem without boats ballasted with people
On the road to the South
A poem without words choked
By the harrows of silence.
The people of the islands want a different poem
For the people of the islands:
A poem with sap rising in the heart of the BEGINNING
A poem with Batuque and tchabeta and the badias of St
    Catherine,
A poem with shaking hips and laughing ivory.
The people of the islands want a different poem
For the people of the islands:
A poem without men who lose the seas' grace
and the fantasy of the main compass points.

The Long Day's March

Onésimo Silveira

All the walls will give way
To the fury of our feet
And no one will falter in the long day's march
Which waits for the blood
To devour the dust on the roads
Drunk with our shouting
We shall darken the landscape from afar
From the penal colonies
We shall at last smile up at the star-light.

Femi-Aura

An insane idiot on the maiden date
set his ears on the solid night
and it happened

that the sound of a passing wind
was his girl
the noise of mating cattle
was his girl
the thunderous sound of flapping lightning
was his girl
the roaring river down the valley
was his girl
the croaking frogs on nuptial season
was his girl
and each time he went to meet his girl in vain
but the girl came
when an angry leopard on a final hunt
roared past the village gate
and kissed the idiot with loving arms
and carried the idiot to a crimson gate.

The Sprinter

I heard your voice
echo
through the reeds

I saw your shadow
float
on the water

I felt your scent
come
through the wind

I saw your image
in the dream

I saw you run on boulder rocks
and laugh
with cattle egrets
and kiss the osaye fruits
and I sprinted
but where were you to be trapped?

Poem in Four Parts

W. Kamera

I

The leaves are withered
Roses fold and shrink.
Dog, the panting athlete shows his tongue.
A dwarfed shadow flees—
Hides under my legs
Nuts wrinkle and crack.

II

The sun is old
The West glows like a worm
Shadows are long
There are cool whispers in the trees
The weavers make for their homes
Old Kibo in his "Kanga" appears.

III

Like honey you covered the lawn
Fleeting beauty—
In the cool of the morning air
Peace-placid and pleasant.

The moist crystals of yesternight
Where are you gone?
I would have you for my own.
Surrendered at the approach of dawn?

IV

Sun from his Eastern cradle
Like a chameleon measures his steps
Stretches his tender arms
Over the silent hills.
The trees exchange greetings
In the gentle whispers of dawn.
The lazy night is over.

The weaverbird disturbs my rest.
Day hatching from the Eastern shell
Uncovers ice-shouldered Kibo.
Life blooms with the rose
In the cool of the morning air
The lazy night is over.

Evening

Stephen Lubega

Never has the death of a poet
Been tolled by all the world.
God's work on earth, though
Has its universal funeral in the west,
Recurrent grave of day's almighty soul.

Never was victory so trumpeted
As that of the sun scorching his fiery way
And then in gorgeous colours falling,
Trailing stars.
Life, death, water and aridity
Bow to his morning ray.

With his passing, death stirs in the thicket.
In church the bell is tolled,
In barracks at the last bugle note
Soldiers like ants file,
The busy woman scolds her child,
Drunkards like sick dogs retch homewards.
The night voice is a harsh guitar.

But on a hill among musizi trees
Sweet nuns sing the litanies
Of the virgin whose Son we know.
Priests like lamp posts in a graveyard
Stoop over the breviary.
There's a piping of crickets in the bush
And a bellowing of frogs—
All sing the ancient elegy
For the sun that has died in the west.

Daybreak

Susan Lwanga

O dawn
Where do you hide your paints at night
That cool breath, that scent,
With which you sweeten the early air?

O dawn
What language do you use
To instruct the birds to sing
Their early songs
And insects to sound
The rhythm of an African heartbeat?

O dawn
Where do you find the good will
To speed the early traffic on its way,
Rouse the cold drunkard
And send your askaris and barking dogs
To chase thieves to their dens?

O dawn
Whose cold breath makes young boys and girls
Glad of a warm sheet,
Enflames the dreams of unmarried ones,
And brings familiar noises
To gladden the hearts of the married.

Sunset

Oswald Mbuyiseni Mtshali

The sun spun like
a tossed coin.
It whirled on the azure sky,
it clattered into the horizon,
it clicked in the slot,
and neon-lights popped
and blinked "Time expired",
as on a parking meter.

Lenrie Peters

Autumn burns me with
primaeval fire. Makes my skin
taut with vague expectation,
hurls me out of summer fatigue
on to a new Bridge of Sighs.

Somewhere I feel the heart
of the earth pumping, and down below
it bleeds in a million ripples.
I drop a sweet memory into
the flow and the cascading grips me with fascination.

Great trees in transit fall
are made naked in langour of shame
solitary like actors on a stage
like stars, orphans, celebrities,
politicians, uncomfortably mysteriously like you and me.

But I will not mourn the sadness.
I will go dead-leaf gathering
for the fire in a slice of sunlight
to fill my lungs with odours of decay
and my eyes with mellowed rainbow colours.

I will go creeping down tasselled
latticed tree-avenues of light
and listen to squirrel tantrums
punctuate the orchestration of autumn silence
and hold in my hand the coiling stuff of nature.

Then I will love
Yes, love; extravagantly under
the flutter of dying leaves
and in a shadow of mist
in wonder; for autumn is wonder and wonder is hope.

Pomegranate

Rabéarivelo

The rays of the new-born sun
   search under the branches
the breast of the ripe pomegranate
   and bite it till it bleeds.

Discreet and shuddering kiss
   hard and scalding embrace.
Soon the pure thrust
   will draw purple blood.

Its taste will be sweeter,
   because it was pregnant with desire
And with fearful love
   and scented blossoms—
Pregnant by the lover sun.

Cactus

Rabéarivelo

That multitude of fused hands
that offer flowers to the sky—
that multitude of fingerless hands

they say a hidden spring
wells from their unbroken palms
that this, its inner source
refreshes myriad herds
and numberless tribes, wandering tribes
in the frontiers of the south.

Fingerless hands from within the spring
Moulded hands, wreathe the sky.

Here,
when the flanks of the city were made as green
as moonbeams glancing through the forests,
when still they cooled the hills of Iarive
crouching like rejuvenated bulls,
upon these rocks, too steep for goats
they hid, to protect their sources,
these lepers that sprouted flowers.

Fathom the cave from which they came
to find the cause of their ravaging sickness
source more shrouded than evening
more distant than dawn—
you will know no more than I.
The blood of the earth, the sweat of stone,
and sperm of the wind,
flushed together within these palms
have melted their fingers
and replaced them with golden flowers.

Daybreak   *Rabéarivelo*

I

Have you ever seen dawn go poaching
in the orchards of night?
Behold her returning
on the pathways of the east

overgrown with flowering speargrass:
head to foot she is splashed with milk
like her children, long suckled by heifers;
and her torch-bearing hands
are black and blue like the lips of a girl
chewing ripe berries.

The birds she has caught in her net escape.
They fly before her.

II

Is it from the east or the west
The first call comes? No one knows
But now the cocks
in their coops transfixed by stars
and other spears of darkness
call to each other
they breathe into seashells
they respond from every side.
And he returns, he
who went to sleep in the ocean,
till the skylark ascending
meets him with songs she carries
drenched with dew.

III

All the stars smelted together
in the crucible of time,
they are chilled in the sea
to a crystal of many facets.
A dying rock, night puts her heart into the task
her yearning is for mill grist
that dissolves, dissolves,
like ashes touched by the wind—
Lovingly she cuts the prism.

The craftsman on his own unnoticed grave
Sets up this monument of light.

Vaulted like the cities of Imerina
that appear on the hills
and cling to the rocks
hunchbacked like the rooftops
which the moon sculpts in the sands;
this is the powerful bull
purple as the colour of his blood.

He has drunk on the river banks
he has grazed on cactus and lilac;
now he crouches before the cassava,
still heavy with the perfume of earth,
and before the rice chaff
whose violent odour infests sun and shadow.

The evening has entrenched everywhere
and the horizon vanishes
The bull sees a desert that extends
to the frontiers of night
His horns are like the crescent
rising.

Desert,
before the powerful bull
desert,
led astray by the evening
into the realm of silence
what images do you evoke
in his half sleep?
Does he see his humpless cousins,
who are red like the dust
that rises behind them;
who are the masters of uninhabited lands?
Or his ancestors, fattened by the peasants
who led them to the city adorned with ripe oranges
to be slain in honour of the king?

He leaps and roars,
he who will die without glory.
He falls asleep, waiting ...
and appears like a mound of earth.

Transformation Scenes   *J. B. Tati-Loutard*

Evening

No more our grave, the sea
Is our antique sarcophagus,
Our remains,
Buried beneath four hundred years of sand
And covered with all the skins of the sky
Ever seen.
Look, the stars are naked
In the bluebed of night;
Clearly seen between their thighs is light;
And the moon climbing to the horizon
Smells all the roses in the colonial garden.

Dawn

All the sea-dogs have deserted this shore
And drowse
Beyond the sun where we believe the dead.
Cradled by the breath of that gentle monsoon
That makes its pilgrimage towards the land,
The lovers caught in four lianas
Weave life again;
And in the rising dawn, the sea,
An old, weary beast of prey,
Treads among the gravel with dove's steps.

Morning

Sea, plant and sun will spring to life again
And all for you.
You will linger on pathways
Where your forefather ran biindly;

Each morning plant wears a pearl of sunlight
In its buttonhole;
You will hear the cricket like a fairy-tale
Left behind under a bush,
In the hard progress of exploration.

XIV
Mating Cry

Phlora

When we first met, it was just by night
in the flowing music in the dance hall
It was my acrobatic feet
on which I lightly swung
that planted a magnet
which caught your eyes on the facade
and the way my tight trousers
caressed the tense air above the floor
I became at once the Ideal
that all years before had dwelt in your dreams
I watched you in that multicoloured dress
and the way you curled your hair
Love itself dwelt there
and only the steel comb woke her up
your feet never did count in my case
only the ivory bangle around your wrist clicked something
and we swore before the band
-that we'd love for ever and a day
Only a few days later
you met that soccer-runner-boxer
who excels at running after nothing
you fell for his chest beef and muscular arms
and swore you'd love him till doomsday
and that in your new game you'd both keep running!
Yet before the cock swallowed a grain of maize
you fell vertically on the concrete floor
at first sight of the guitarist at the club
he was cute and angelic
and you advised the former one
I mean the athletic lad
that henceforth he could walk in life
And, Phlora, you just deserted him
just in matter of seconds you broke the whole fabric
of all the athletic prowess
You picked up in a flash
a rebellious undergraduate

but they came home the other day
after rioting
and you swore you'd pair him in life
But Phlo you have just deserted him
on hearing of his untimely expulsion
since you sentenced him a failure in life's contest
Life itself Phlora
is densely clouded with thick outgrowths of thorns
Through your mirror
you see him derailed and capsized
closing your eyes to the new track under construction
down that drain where he has fallen
down where he has plunged
I hear later you cajoled into submission
that beefy unsexy minister
'cos he was a responsible man
whose future was clear and promising
that future was full of assets
all the historical ravages were but liabilities
yet Phlo you discarded the whims of elections
for in a twilight he lost his deposit
and out was swept that brilliant future
he stood in the cold with naught save
the junior Certificate of Education
that was of no use to prospective employers
Now you wish and wish and wish
but wishes dwindle and flicker into unknown
Why do you wish you never derailed men?
That you never sifted them in an unsifted sift
today you see more clearly in a niggled background
that Wisdom swore to follow
the path trodden by foolishness
Wishing-to-know never comes first
today you'll see future spread out on the field
where once you ran chasing nothing nothing but love
see it spread as wide as the sky
you'll never see its contents
the countless defendants

gnaw sharp teeth on each edge
Phlo veer sharply around fortune
kinked paths await you all along
chunks of rocks fall from unknown
and love was a bargain for the best
Today look at the accepted history
and assess the properties of love
if one is not Abstract Pretence
for people who deem it an asset.

The Mesh

Kwesi Brew

We have come to the cross-roads
And I must either leave or come with you.
I lingered over the choice
But in the darkness of my doubts
You lifted the lamp of love
And I saw in your face
The road that I should take.

Dennis Brutus

In the friendly dark, I wheel
as a bird checks in flight
to glide down streams
and planes of slanting air

so I turn, worn by work
and the dull teeth of care
to find your face, your throat
and the soft dark of your hair;

flesh lies snugged in sheets
the brain, wrapped close in folds
of the still-blanketing night,
awaits the easy balm of dreams,

but my heart soars and wheels
hurtling through the friendly dark
to find your mouth and your heart
and nest quietly there.

Dennis Brutus

Let not this plunder be misconstrued:
This is the body's expression of need—
Poor wordless body in its fumbling way
Exposing heart's-hunger by raiding and hurt;

    Secret recesses of lonely desire
    Gnaw at the vitals of spirit and mind
    When shards of existence display eager blades
    To menace and savage the pilgriming self:

Bruised though your flesh and all-aching my arms
Believe me, my lovely, I too reel from our pain—
Plucking from you these your agonized gifts
Bares only my tenderness-hungering need.

Dennis Brutus

The rosy aureole of your affection
extends beyond our urban bounded knowledge
to tangled undergrowths of earlier time:
subtly obscure lymphatics of the flesh
proliferate bright labyrinths of mind
and cobweb-shadow them with primal dusk.

Beyond our focused shaped projection
to immensities of tenderness defined
like blind protrusion of these searching nipple
shut-eyed in luminous rooms of lust I nuzzle,
loom shadows darker than the dusk of passion
that turn our pinks dust-grey as spider's back.

Beyond your open hungering embrace
yawn other older mouths from oozy shores
and over me, enormous, straddles
the ancient foetus-hungry incubus
that leaves me sprawling, spent, discarded
dry-sucked and shattered as a spider's shard.

Dennis Brutus

It is the constant image of your face
framed in my hands as you knelt before my chair
the grave attention of your eyes
surveying me amid my world of knives
that stays with me, perennially accuses
and convicts me of heart's-treachery;
and neither you nor I can plead excuses
for you, you know, can claim no loyalty—
my land takes precedence of all my loves.

Yet I beg mitigation, pleading guilty
for you, my dear, accomplice of my heart
made, without words, such blackmail with your beauty
and proffered me such dear protectiveness
that I confess without remorse or shame
my still-fresh treason to my country
and hope that she, my other, dearest love
will pardon freely, not attaching blame
being your mistress (or your match) in tenderness.

Siriman Cissoko

I

O tulip, tulip I have chosen from among all the flowers of our
    great races of men!
I sing your slim black body, I tell of your slender girl's body,
    of your suddenly flashing eyes

I cry aloud the blue palm tree of your lashes
The broadswords of your plaited tresses, commas of lightning
    stabbing the sky.
I shout your charms, ah! your lips that are fleshy dates!

II

Young woman, full bosomed, loins more fertile than the banks
    of the Nile
I will wait for you when in my vast orchards the mangoes like
    censers breathe out their smells;
And the wind sways the great fans and most delicate gifts.
Then, on an evening of bairam, very early you will come,
    O beauty of blackness, under your white veil.
I will welcome you among wedding songs and rhapsodies of
    blood.
I will be clothed all in dream, but no mirror in my hut
Only the green of your eyes where I may drown my longing.
I will gird me with the strength of the young men to carry yo
    off more swiftly leaving the impatient matrons without.
Woi! You will be my glory, I your pride, O Beauty of blackn

III

Sope, when you are gay, when you are gay, my Sope
Your smile caresses my eyes.

Then I would become your joy, to unfold your tulip face.
Yes, die upon your lips, quench myself in your voice,
Yes, drown in your dark eyes.

When my dark lady walks, the desire takes me to be under he
    feet.
That I might kiss her feet, that they might trample my heart,
    ah! Lord!

When my dark lady adorns herself, she is Sogolon, the Malinke
    Princess.
Would I were boubou, jewels, golden slippers.

Between my fingers, from thread and from gold and from leather
Let me weave her body in finest diamonds, in my glittering
    poems.

Black Rain

Keki Darwul

I cannot cry like you
shoulders hunched into a knot of pain
and the face breaking into a thousand pieces.
I must stand erect, my eyes
spaceless and open; too much thinking
against the cold wind and they may think
I am holding back tears.

I must live with my grief
As a stone breaker lives with his vocation;
must feed them on the thirteenth day on plantain leaves.
go to the office with a shaved head,
hang my coat on a peg and pretend
that nothing has happened.

The roles are reversed is a way
. . . not exactly for that would look stage-managed . . .
but others are crying around you today
As I live ash sizzles on the cold river
like a dying passion
it takes all the strength in me
to restrain a shiver;
And yet with all the cold despair around
this sterile moment oozing this black rain
I envy you the quiver
with which your tears came
and your relief.

As for me, grey hair-roots
sprouting from the scalp next week
may be my only catharsis.

Akosua 'Nowa   *Joe de Graft*

They say the guinea-fowl lays her treasure
Where only she can find it.
Akosua 'Nowa is a guinea-fowl:
Go tell her, red ant upon the tree.

I met Akosua 'Nowa this morning;
I greeted:
  Akosua, how is your treasure?
She looked me slowly up and down,
She sneered:
  The man is not yet here who'll find it!

Akosua 'Nowa has touched my manhood;
Tell her, red ant upon the tree:
If she passes this way I am gone,
I am gone to load my gun.

No matter how hidden deep her treasure,
By my father's coffin I swear
I'll shoot my way to it this day;
Son of the hunter king
  There is liquid fire in my gun!

Shifting Gears   *Solomon Deressa*

I who swim
In the stealth of a dream
Listening to the mind's insane silence scream,
Because of colour lack
I shall paint your loving face
In colourless breath,
With grapnel-fingers in an empty colour rack,
Beneath the quiet curve of your lashes
Two simple awesome dots in black,

You whose love never wavered
Towards whom I forever crack
On the tip of my parched tongue.

Compassion

Mbella Sonne Dipoko

Already tomorrow's rhythm is rising
On the hills flanking the long river.

Although we may disappear like the wind in antipodal nests
We shall return
Being like birds that come and go.

Do you remember the big moon
Bowl-like flower unfolding from the clouds that spread before us
Like a dark field?

In the Isère
The misery of nocturnal sobbing drowned
While our breathing mixed with the mountain's respiration
And we planted our words like kites
In the soft ridges of time.

A new spring was born that evening
As the sky crowned the beloved with a halo of lunar lilacs.

The Echoes

Mazisi Kunene

Over the vast summer hills
I shall commission the maternal sun
To fetch you with her long tilted rays,

The slow heave of the valleys
Will once again roll the hymns of accompaniment
Scattering the glitter of the milky way over the bare fields.

You will meet me
Underneath the shadow of the timeless earth
Where I lie weaving the seasons.

You will indulge in the sway dances of your kin
To the time of symphonic flutes
Ravishing the identity of water lilies.

I have opened the mountain gates
So that the imposing rim
Of the Ruwenzori shall steal your image.

Even the bubbling lips of continents
(To the shy palms of Libya)
Shall awake the long-forgotten age.

The quivering waters of the Zambezi river
Will bear on a silvery blanket your name
Leading it to the echoing of the sea.

Let me not love you alone
Lest the essence of your being
Lie heavy on my tongue
When you count so many to praise.

Woman   *Valente Malangatana*

In the cool waters of the river
we shall have fish that are huge
which shall give the sign of
the end of the world perhaps
because they will make an end of woman
woman who adorns the fields
woman who is the fruit of man.

The flying fish makes an end of searching
because woman is the gold of man
when she sings she even seems

like the fado-singer's well-tuned guitar
when she dies, I shall cut off
her hair to deliver me from sin.

Woman's hair shall be the blanket
over my coffin when another Artist
calls me to Heaven to paint me
Woman's breasts shall be my pillow
woman's eye shall open up for me the way to Heaven
woman's belly shall give birth to me up there
and woman's glance shall watch me
as I go up to Heaven.

Joy Cry

Arthur Nortje

Apollo's man-breasts smooth and gold-blond
hold between in the fine-boned cleft
the kernel of radiant light. Like wind
youth's madness streams through the orifices. The swift
vivacious morning shoots along the ripples:
in my loins the swelling pearl moves.

This growing jewel wants to burst
through coils and meshes the seasons have wrought.
That time can tame the green surge,
that age can quell the riotous blood,
my eyes, blind with their glory, shun.
The snow-melt waters roar down the mountain.

The joy cry of virility stirs quivers:
from your navel I bite the ivory flower.
Bud-firm, you have opened under thunder,
in your galleries my shapeless flame would dwell.
So I shall soothe your tender wound,
the one that's life-long, and unhealable.

Promise   *Arthur Nortje*

Clock and season march, each day more mellow.
since time must nourish youth beyond blossoms:
the new furred power glints in early patterns,
brought with true focus to your beauty now.

Words drift in multitudes from your replies,
who've chosen foreign life: I ponder snatches.
We crossed like shadows, young and watchful insects.
My time has turned to life beyond this room.

All loves have love-songs, once a girl well thought of
set spinning a lugubrious Italian.
You, mermaid with your criss-cross rain of pale
hair, never had favourites, just friends.

That sweet detachment lingers rich in influence.
O day beyond the curtain swarms with rhythms.
My song to you is imminent: sky and glittering
sea and the grass of quick surprise, our world.

The luminous air presents its gifts of fragrance,
myself with its first taste in flowering spring.
The wind strays off the water with desire
among these leafing boughs to fork me open.

As I grow outward, what has held me shut,
unconscious of your vigil, you my swan?
I am as strong and fluid as a river
to give your empty spring its first fulfilment

Rhythm of the Pestle   *Richard Ntiru*

Listen—listen—
listen to the palpable rhythm
of the periodic pestle,
plunging in proud perfection

into the cardial cavity
of maternal mortar
like the panting heart
of the virgin bride
with the silver hymen,
or the approaching stamp
of late athleting cows
hurrying home to their bleating calves.

At each succeeding stroke
the grain darts, glad to be scattered
by the hard glint
of the pestle's passion.

During the aerial suspension
of the pendent pestle
the twice-asked, twice-disappointed girl
thinks of the suitor that didn't come,
of her who dragged her name through ashes
uncleansed by the goat-sacrifice,
of her bridal bed
that vanished with the ephemeral dream,
of her twin firstlings
that will never be born,
and her weltering hands
grip, grip, rivet hard
and downright down
comes the vengeance pestle.

I have seen the hearth
and the triplets,
but no trace of ash . . .

Now the grain jumps, reluctantly,
each time lower and lower,
smiling the half-white smile
of the teething baby,
glad to be crushed,

glad to be sublimated
to the quintessential powder
after the consummation.

In the bananas
the girls dance, singing of one
who saw her father in sleepy drunkenness
and confided in the birds of the sky.

Still the perennial pestle
pounds the tribulations of a battered soul
and the caked countenance of an orphaned age
to the intensity and fineness
of a powder.

Without You   *Odia Ofeimun*

In your absence
my life is all a stammer
hunted down
by a non-existent tomorrow

I feel guilty
of sins I have not committed
borne on the wings
of incessant fears

Without you,
my earth suffers a demise of colours
as when a guest leaves a house
at night
the light goes out

After the Photograph

Nothing will suffice, save your
animal presence.

This angelic impression you send down
to rejuvenate my chagrined battery
exudes a tang of incarnate purity
But—

You must not suppose you have done
my anguished longing for warmth
to peace;
            Rather
you whet the leopard's claw
of the loneliness which derides
the humour of these days.

Heckled to a knowledge
of having what I cannot hold
—an infant lizard, monsters, remorse,
in my lack of grasp—
I dare say

You must edge the canoehead
of your concern
to the littorals of the gathering dusks
where your smile will build for me
summers to tame the wild urges
of these superlative doubts

O nothing will suffice, save your
animal presence.

Sleep
    not
        on the sleeping
Wall—
        come sleep
On my
        shoulder;
                    why do
You
    prefer
The wall
        to my human
Shoulder? it
May be coldly
                tall, but
I am
    near
And fonder;
            I have sent
You
    the call,
            wishing to
Be
    the sole
Holder
        of the head
                    that
Will fall
        from
Your neck
            whose moulder
                        has
Given
    me
You—
        and all
            for now till

When
>> we grow

Older;
>> sleep not
>>>> on the

Sleeping wall—
Come sleep on my shoulder.

Lenrie Peters

Love is juxtaposed to the Ego,
competes with the Ego;
stands between it and life
like a dark photographic screen, inverted;
terrifies with rat-tailed ambience
as the French and Pagans use it,
nibbles at resistance with haze of spectroscopic light.
At cellular level
a mutilation of stress fractures
ensure dangerous alteration of mood and shape;
escape narrows the gaps,
makes solid ground—imprisons pain
of sharp modality.
A tight fermenting nucleus
procreates and dies;
and each exploded fragment
punctures the flesh, wrings out the nerves
drives somnolence from the eyes.
The bones glow with rubbing as cave men knew,
and soul distilled in tears
does not assuage the yearning or fears.
Yet through the cloudy maceration
a Gossamer line of destiny
transmits the rapture of danger
into a flowered eternity of years.

There you stand
erect and naked
you are a lime tree and remember;
but truly you are the child of this fertile shadow
that feeds on lunar milk;
slowly you take the shape of a pillar
on this low wall over which dreams of flowers drift
and the perfume of a relaxed summer.

To feel to believe that roots sprout at your feet
and move and twist themselves like thirsty snakes
towards some underground source
or that they clench the sand
and make you part of it, you, living one,
unknown tree, unnamed tree
that develops fruit
which you must pluck yourself.

A crown,
in your hair dishevelled by the wind,
conceals a nest of transcendent birds,
and when you will come to sleep in my bed,
and I will recognize you, my errant brother,
your touch, your breath, and the odour of your skin
will provoke the rustling of mysterious winds
even to the frontiers of sleep.

The Return
Arnaldo Santos

Colourless banners
Trembling in the wind

A truck passes and voices sing
    —men going home

The full song carries far
To scattered huts where mothers wait

Banner-desires
Trembling in the wind

And voices left traced on the matting floor
Like the dust of the streets
Their songs of parting

And ever trembling
Colourless banners arouse desires

In the townships, new babies' cries are formed.

L. S. Senghor

(for flutes)
A hand of light caressed my eyelids of darkness
And your smile rose like the sun on the mists drifting grey and
    cold over my Congo.
My heart has echoed the virgin song of the dawn-birds
As my blood kept time once to the white song of the sap in the
    branches of my arms.
See, the bush flower and the star in my hair, and the band
    round the forehead of the herdsman athlete.
I will take the flute, I will make a rhythm for the slow peace
    of the herds
And all day sitting in the shade of your eyelashes, close to the
    Fountain of Fimla,
I shall faithfully pasture the flaxen lowings of your herds.
For this morning a hand of light caressed my eyelids of darkness
And all day long my heart has echoed the virgin song of the
    birds.

L. S. Senghor

(for khalam)

I came with you as far as the village of grain-huts, to the gates
of Night

I had no words before the golden riddle of your smile.

A brief twilight fell on your face, freak of the divine fancy.

From the top of the hill where the light takes refuge, I saw the
brightness of your cloth go out

And your crest like a sun dropped beneath the shadow of the
ricefields

When the anxieties came against me, ancestral fears more
treacherous than panthers

—The mind cannot push them back across the day's horizons.

Is it then night for ever, parting never to meet again?

I shall weep in the darkness, in the motherly hollow of the Earth

I will sleep in the silence of my tears

Until my forehead is touched by the milky dawning of your
mouth.

L. S. Senghor

(for khalam)

Long, long have you held between your hands the black face
of the warrior

Held as if already there fell on it a twilight of death.

From the hill I have seen the sun set in the bays of your eyes.

When shall I see again, my country, the pure horizon of your
face?

When shall I sit down once more at the dark table of your
breast?

Hidden in the half-darkness, the nest of gentle words.

I shall see other skies and other eyes

I shall drink at the spring of other mouths cooler than lemons

I shall sleep under the roof of other heads of hair in shelter
from storms.

But every year, when the rum of springtime sets my memory ablaze,
I shall be full of regret for my homeland and the rain from your eyes on the thirsty savannahs.

L. S. Senghor

-(*for khalam*)

Is it surprising my dear if my melody has become sombre
If I have laid aside the smooth reed for the khalam and tama
And the green smell of the ricefields for the grumbling of the drums?

Listen to the menace of the old men — diviners, cannonade of wrath of God.
Ah! perhaps tomorrow the crimson voice of your dyali will cease for ever.
That is the reason my rhythm has grown so urgent my fingers bleed on my khalam.

Perhaps tomorrow my dear I shall fall on an unappeased soil
Full of regret for your setting eyes, and the misty drumbeat of the pounding in the mortars back home.
And in the dusk you will be full of regret for the burning voice that sang once of your dark beauty.

L. S. Senghor

(*for two flutes*)

I have spun a song soft as a murmur of doves at noon
To the shrill notes of my four-stringed khalam.
I have woven you a song and you did not hear me.
I have offered you wild flowers with scents as strange as a sorcerer's eyes
I have offered you my wild flowers. Will you let them wither,
Finding distraction in the mayflies dancing?

L. S. Senghor

(for two flutes and a distant drum)

Was it a Mograbin night? I leave Mogador with its Platinum
    daughters.

Was it a Mograbin night? It was also the Night our night of
    Joal

Before we were born, inexpressible night: you did up your hair
    in the mirror of my eyes.

We sat anxiously in the shadow of our secret

Anxiously waiting and your nostrils quivered.

Do you remember that noise of peace? from the lower town,
    wave upon wave

Till it was breaking at our feet. In the distance a lighthouse
    called to my right

To my left, next to my heart, the strange immobility of your
    eyes.

These sudden flashes of lightning in the night of the rainy
    season—I could read your face

And I took long parched draughts of your terrible face and
    they inflamed my thirst

And in my astonished heart in my heart of silence in my
    nonplussed heart

Those gusts of barking down there that burst it like a grenade.

Then the bronze crunch of sand, the leaves flickered like eyelids.

The black guards passed by, giant gods of Eden: moon-faced
    moths

Rested gently on their arms—their happiness scalded us.

Listening to our hearts, we heard them beating down there at
    Fadioutt

We heard the earth tremble under the conquering feet of the
    athletes

And the voice of the Beloved singing the shadowy splendour
    of the Lover.

And if the eagle suddenly flung itself at our breast, with a
  Comet's fierce cry?
But the irresistible current carried me away towards the
horrible song of the reefs of your eyes.

There will be other nights my dear. You will come again to
sit in this bank of shadow
You will aways be same and you will not be the same.
Does it matter? Through all your transformations, I shall
  Worship the features of Koubma Tam.

Serenade   Traditional (From the Swahili)

O lady, be calm and cry not but sing to your suitors
Sing to those who guide you and to the discerning
passers-by,
  Sorrow and distress.
O lady, be calm, let me give you gifts, fine clothes from our
  Homeland the Hejaz
Let me adorn you with a chain and beads of gold devised in
  Shiraz
Let me build for you a great white house of lime and stone.
Let me furnish it for you with furnishings of crystal that
those
  Who see it shall sing its praise.
Spread beneath with rushes soft from the lake-sides of
Shaka and Ozi
Lat me satisfy your good parents and let them rest at case
with mainstrels' sogns
Let them lie at case with food fo young camels and of oxen,
  Sheep and goats
Because, my lady, O lady mine let me tell you, you are my
  Beloved.

Love Song   *Traditional (from the Amharic)*

You lime of the forest, honey among the rocks,
Lemon of the cloister, grape in the savannah.
A hip to be enclosed by one hand;
A thigh round like a piston.
Your back—a manuscript to read hymns from.
Your eye triggerhappy, shoots heroes.
Your gown cobweb-tender,
Your shirt like soothing balm.
Soap? O no, you wash in Arabian scent,
Your calf painted with silver lines.
I dare not touch you!
Hardly dare to look back.
You mistress of my body:
More precious to me than my hand or my foot.
Like the fruit of the valley, the water of paradise.
Flower of the sky; wrought by divine craftsmen;
With muscular thigh she stepped on my heart
Her eternal heel trod me down.
But have no compassion with me:
Her breast resembles the finest gold;
When she opens her heart—
The Saviour's image!
And Jerusalem herself, sacred city,
Shouts "Holy, holy!"

XV
Mortality

The Journey Beyond

Kofi Awoonor

The bowling cry through door posts
carrying boiling pots
ready for the feasters.
Kutsiami the benevolent boatman;
when I come to the river shore
please ferry me across
I do not have on my cloth-end
the price of your stewardship.

Elegy for my friend E. Galo

Mazisi Kunene

You died without my knowing
When I was out collecting firewood
To roast the meat,
That we may dance over the earth,
Even with white fat oxen;
And dance, not caring for the shape of their horns.
You died without my knowing,
When I thought I would tell you stories
Saying "once upon a time on the earth"—
Meaning we who are one with the years
Meaning the beating of the hearts
Beating against the muscles of their desires.
I bought them expensively with gold.
You died without my knowing
You covered me with shame
As I followed you,
Admonishing those who carried you
Not to imitate you
And say death is a common thing.
If it were true I would not be here,
I would not have known that locusts
Greedily reap the fields
Leaving the discordant symphony of naked stars.
It is these that wept over the centuries.

For a Friend who was killed in the War

Mazisi Kunene

Single Voice:	In the sun-drenched cliffs of the evening
	Where I bade my brother farewell.
Group:	Birds beat their wings and turn away.
Single Voice:	I should not have returned alive
Group:	The heart weeps endlessly.
Single Voice:	It would have been you facing this fatal grief.
All:	The worlds have scars, the worlds weep.
Single Voice:	Even the dreams that I dream fill me with fear.
All:	The leopard devours whom it chooses,
	It is now I experience the grief of widows.
Single Voice:	How shall I report at the house of Somhlalela?
	How shall I?

Lenrie Peters

The panic
of growing older
spreads fluttering wings
from year to year

At twenty
stilled by hope
of gigantic success
time and exploration

At thirty
a sudden throb of
pain. Laboratory tests
have nothing to show

Legs cribbed
in domesticity allow
no sudden leaps
at the moon now

Copybook bisected
with red ink
and failures—
nothing to show the world

Three children perhaps
the world expects
it of you. No
specialist's effort there.

But science gives hope
of twice three score
and ten. Hope
is not a grain of sand.

Inner satisfaction
dwindles in sharp
blades of expectation.
From now on the world has you.

Lenrie Peters

You lie there naked
though shrouds obscure your face.
Your body hairs shaved,
underlines your numerical fate.

Blue anaesthetic fumes
rise, float, encircle your brain
dreaming, nothing but sand dunes;
outside the hapless patter of rain

A stranger hovers over you
himself protected, hidden from view—
the scalpel trembles in his hand
heavy with the passage of years.

All is controlled, serene
a sharp light penetrates your skin
illuminates your gross disease
deeper than your consciousness of sin.

The Metronome alters the beat
methodically he dissects
like a swallow building a nest
with every defiance of death.

A jet of blood a bead of sweat
pain in the chest, the scherzo ends.
Foul abuse spatters the walls
a maniac rummages your sceptred halls.

You lie there naked
asleep through a tropical storm
when you wake
the puddles like your disease have gone.

No use shouting for help
this lonely man. Only he knows
the horrors of your faked anatomy
the conflict of heaven and hell.

The tension eases with the last stitch
he forces a joke to make amends
he has crossed it before—this ditch
and all the passion he expends.

Tomorrow by your bedside
cool as frozen plaice
you will not see it in his face
this stranger with the scalpel from outer space.

Watching someone die
is a fraudulent experience
The deep significance I felt
the meaning escapes
like a child's first punishment.
The dying ravish your strength
whether by throttle of convulsive gasp
or tideless fading away
like ancient familiar sounds in sea shells
the moment is the same
reinforced brutality to life
a rugged cliff bloodstained
with the agonizing rhythm of many heads,
A cold demise; each
successive moment a banishment.
The terror is in leaving behind
the ache is in departing.

Humming phantasies crowd their strings
to seize and record the moment
the hands curl in spasm
to hold it back; this life, this infidel.
It is too late. Everything and nothing
has happened. A huge machine
the earth, grinds to a bolt-knocking halt.

It is the changing of the tide
at the boundary hour
Life like a handful of feathers
engulfed by cliff winds
one like yourself swept
oh so swiftly into the anchorage of History
Tears and sighs sighs and tears
stamping the leaden feet
the solid agony of years
they all abound

one life or a million
contrived by nature or man
greatly obscures the issue.
Face to face with dying
you are none-the-wiser
Yet it seems a most ignoble epitaph
"He was a man and had to die; after all."

To My First White Hairs
Wole Soyinka

Hirsute hell chimney-spouts, black thunderthroes
confluence of coarse cloudfleeces—my head sir!—scourbrush
in bitumen, past fossil beyond fingers of light—until . . .!

Sudden sprung as corn stalk after rain, watered milk weak;
as lightning shrunk to ant's antenna, shrivelled
off the febrile sight of crickets in the sun—

THREE WHITE HAIRS! frail invaders of the undergrowth
interpret time. I view them, wired wisps, vibrant coiled
beneath a magnifying glass, milk-thread presages

Of the hoary phase. Weave then, weave o quickly weave
your sham veneration. Knit me webs of winter sagehood,
nightcap, and the fungoid sequins of a crowr

Post Mortem
Wole Soyinka

there are more functions to a freezing plant
than stocking beer; cold biers of mortuaries
submit their dues, harnessed—glory be!—

in the cold hand of death . . .
his mouth was cotton filled, his man-pike
shrunk to sub-soil grub

his head was hollowed and his brain
on scales—was this a trick to prove
fore-knowledge after death?

his flesh confesses what has stilled
his tongue; masked fingers think from him
to learn, how not to die.

let us love all things of grey; grey slabs
grey scalpel, one grey sleep and form,
grey images.

Traditional (from the Yoruba)

The hunter dies
and leaves his poverty to his gun.
The blacksmith dies
and leaves his poverty to his anvil.
The farmer dies
and leaves his poverty to his hoe.
The bird dies
and leaves its poverty to its nest.
You have died
and left me abandoned in the dark.
Where are you now?
Are you the goat
eating grass round the house?
Are you the motionless lizard
on the hot mud wall?
If, I tell you not to eat earthworms
it's like asking you to go hungry.
But whatever they may eat in heaven—
Partake with them.
A dead body cannot receive double punishment:
If there is not cloth to cover it—
there will always be earth to cover it.

Traditional (from the Yoruba)

Slowly the muddy pool becomes a river.
Slowly my mother's illness becomes her death.
When wood breaks, it can be mended.
But ivory breaks for ever.
An egg falls to reveal a messy secret.
My mother went and carried her secret along.
She has gone far—
We look for her in vain.
But when you see the kob antelope on the way to the farm,
When you see the kob antelope on the way to the river—
leave your arrows in the quiver,
and let the dead depart in peace.

Leaf in the Wind

Bernard Dadié

I am the man the colour of Night
Leaf in the wind, I go at the drift of my dreams.

I am the tree budding in spring
The dew that hums in the baobab's hollow.

Leaf in the wind, I go at the drift of my dreams.

I am the man they complain of
Because opposed to formality
The man they laugh at
Because opposed to barriers.

Leaf in the wind, I go at the drift of my dreams.

I am the man they talk about:
  "Oh him!"
Him you cannot hold
The breeze that touches you and is gone

Leaf in the wind, I go at the drift of my dreams

Captain at the stern
Scanning the scudding clouds
For the earth's powerful eye;
Ship without sail
That glides on the sea.

Leaf in the wind, I go at the drift of my dreams

I am the man whose dreams
Are manifold as the stars
More murmurous than swarms of bees
More smiling than children's smiles
More sonorous than echoes in the woods.

Leaf in the wind, I go at the drift of my dreams.

Seven Sides and Seven Syllables

for Aimé Césaire and Pierre Emmanuel

Edouard J. Maunick

I

happen you come on your own
to this contradicted place
re-celebrate ebony
the original metal

> happen you essay the dream
> before you outlive yourself
> before the blood surges back
> before your father expires

this land once was a mirror
which was silvered by the sea
in the sweat of oars, islands
with keys girded up their loins

> good fortune surrounded us
> in no way surprising us
> if we wager on the sea
> for the last possible time

but what can be the last time
for the deracinated?
again, those who oppose him
share the flesh of the poet

> unaware, he keeps going
> not heeding all the mad ways
> all countries merge dizzily
> in this country of his own

II

my love is improbable
let the saliva well up

neutrality, its token
skimming the garden of birth

> here the roses are roses
> sword-lilies prohibited
> a man who speaks standing up
> has his eyes bandaged with rain

we all take powerful root
on assassination day
with the garden's iron pickets
stained bright by the equinox

> here a man who speaks standing
> is submerged in thé symbol:
> I say rose and it means hope
> but who will live by this game?

who will take up sword-lilies
in their form of machetes
to knot up with blood once more
what survives as a mongrel?

> the whole world I name garden
> I leave no place unbaptizéd
> who will plant garden fences
> if not I, or my kin-folk?

I, the child of all races
soul of India, Europe,
my identity branded
in the cry of Mozambique

III

> thus I am anonymous
> while holding the heritage
> of your ancestral truncheons
> and your black man's evasions

I could accept your labels
and stay unidentified
be tattooed by your numbers
while remaining uncounted

command all your battlements
cloak myself in your panic
recognizing the thunder
and recognizing the wind

know the substance of exile:
on the sea, wind and thunder
recognizing all roots
of the tree that rejects me

recognizing all the roots
tongue-ties me with bereavement
on the shores of denial
I will choose to be Negro

I've read Senghor and Césaire
and Guillen and Richard Wright
but Lorea and St John Perse
Dylan Thomas and Cadou

Paul Eluard, vertical
all reinvent memory
you step out of the mirror
to marry morning with night

IV
rising in me, the promise:
my mouth will spit bitterness
to crack the rejecting rock
at the end of all stanzas

utterance moves towards a place
where snow, thunder cohabit

of words fouled by long weeping
of visions searing the skin

with desires pure and bitter
tumultuous silences
I here spell out my poem
releasing my love of you

        withholding what must be said
        dividing my blood from blood
        inhabiting somewhere else
        than the habitable space

exile is no easy thing
despite obscure boundaries
open doors and living hands
no, it is never easy!

        to accept is to refuse
        refusal reveals anger
        fling open your registers!
        bring your mortal crucifix!

I swear to understand flesh
transparent as lake water
I shall murder ancient seas
set fire to their slave cargoes

V

        CHRIST, but the odour of chains
        and this rattling of metal
        against the defeated bones
        these quincunxes of ropes!

I can force my eyes to see
but the sight is too tragic:
dogs trained to attack the blacks
and their spirituals stabbed

yes, to watch the capsizing
of woman and child voices
whose offence is vertical
because they refuse to crawl

is this Christmas and manger?
are these our poems pure white?
are these our poems deep black?
this the summation of poems?

VI

what right have I to denounce
while shooting with your own guns?
or healing with your own hands?
I freeze and starve for us all

if I could find a kingdom
between midday and midnight
I would go forth and proclaim
my mixed blood to the core

for I choose the you-in-me
without colour or passport
they say we all long for God
and we are all forgiven

VII

happen you come on your own
to this contradicted place
to embrace the bitter dream
of the solar boundaries

discover the point of light
which is the true equator
having no need of the sea
to conceal your departures

happen you come without wrath
to this place of denial
open your eyes to the rain
leave the body till it splits

at last, for a final time
adjust your steps to the steps
of the sole presence in you:
a man the size of a man

my love may only exist
when endorsed by your absence
I no longer need the past
to stand up in the present

the *manèges* of the sea
are not mad *manèges* now
I had to silence my fate
with this, my derisive voice.

High and Low   *Oswald Mbuyiseni Mtshali*

Glorious is this world,
the world that sustains man
like a maggot in a carcase

Mighty is the sea
de-salted by the carapace in the eye of a fish.

Hallowed is the star,
effulgent in the firmament,
a pearl in the stomach of a mussel sky.

Majestic soars the eagle, golden winged above the low life.

Black is the hole of the poet,
a mole burrowing from no entrance to no exit.

For Chinua Achebe

Odia Ofeimun

You say your hurricane lamp can issue
no more the perfunctory flame
of artistic innocence.
(Ostrich mentalities, you have seen,
will not help the situation.)
I raise my fist to your guts

The strafing reports, the "assault and battery"
of questions which splinter our snailshells
decide us in their maledictory exercise.
For, none can afford the lyrical sanity
of the hermit when his clothes are on fire

I raise my fist to your guts

But, then, when troubadours become matchets
in the frenzy of storms they must underline,
their finest truths are iron banners
to wrap the corpses of fleeting slogans

And, Compatriot, this is my concern . . .

I suppose you can break the kernel of these days
better than my poor plastic slab will allow
You know the intricate weave of the barbwire-roost
into which you must plunge

Oh, my concern overpowers me;
I do not know how to escape from
such wind as bear you, now, away
from your, once, unruffled waters

Heavensgate

I The Passage

Before you, mother Idoto,*
    naked I stand;
before your watery presence,
    a prodigal

leaning on an oilbean,
lost in your legend.

Under your power wait I
    on barefoot,
watchman for the watchword
    at *Heavensgate*;

out of the depths my cry:
give ear and hearken . . .

Dark waters of the beginning.

Rays, violet and short, piercing the gloom,
foreshadow the fire that is dreamed of.

Rainbow on far side, arched like boa bent to kill,
foreshadows the rain that is dreamed of.

Me to the orangery
solitude invites,
a wagtail, to tell
the tangled-wood-tale;
a sunbird, to mourn
a mother on a spray.

Rain and sun in single combat;
on one leg standing,

* A village stream. The oilbean, the tortoise and the python are totems
for her worship.

in silence at the passage,
the young bird at the passage.

Silent faces at crossroads:
 festivity in black . . .

Faces of black like long black
 column of ants,

behind the bell tower,
into the hot garden
where all roads meet:
festivity in black . . .

O Anna at the knobs of the panel oblong,
hear us at crossroads at the great hinges

where the players of loft pipe organs
rehearse old lovely fragments, alone—

strains of pressed orange leaves on pages,
bleach of the light of years held in leather:

For we are listening in cornfields
 among the windplayers,
listening to the wind leaning over
 its loveliest fragment . . .

V   Newcomer
Time for worship—

softly sing the bells of exile,
 the angelus,
softly sings my guardian angel.

Mask over my face—

my own mask, not ancestral—I sing:
remembrance of calvary,
and of age of innocence, which is of . . .

Time for worship:

ANNA OF THE PANEL OBLONGS,
   PROTECT ME
FROM THEM FUCKING ANGELS:
   PROTECT ME
MY SANDHOUSE AND BONES.

FOR GEORGETTE

In the chill breath of the day's waking
comes the newcomer,

when the draper of May
has sold out fine green garments,

and the hillsides have made up their faces,
and the gardens, on their faces a painted smile:

such synthetic welcome at the cock's third siren;
when from behind the bulrushes

waking, in the teeth of the chill May morn
comes the newcomer.

I am standing above the noontide,
above the bridgehead;

listening to the laughter of waters
   that do not know why:

listening to incense —

I am standing above the noontide
   with my head above it;

under my feet flat the waters
tide blows them under . . .

Lenrie Peters

Mine is the silent face
in the railway compartment
    in the queue
My flesh is drowsy with paint
    hideously faint
I travel through desperate
deserted places, my life
    ends in you vacantly
an empty tin rolling down
    catty cobbled alleys

I know the strength of the wind
in anger and the passion of waves
    —no floating mermaids—
Standing as I do
as all do
at the cutting chaotic edge of things
my youth burrows into the yearning
entrails of earth; dessicated.

A blank image stares out of flames
out of a dense affluent tomorrow
    studded with blame.
I tear at toasted locks of sunlight
reeds, parched reeds creaking in my lungs
It takes my life to hold the moon in focus.

Crushing dead glass in my strong hand
is worthless. Nothing bleeds, nothing relieves
it will not melt like snow
this emptiness, this hell I invented.

Turning the pages of my diary slowly
But rationally under candle light
Halting over entries of bare folly
And the many words I did not write

The sudden shock of scattered references
And "to be developed" signs
Jotted with unwholesome sentences
And ill-developed rhymes

Pages fastened with candle grease and ink
Remind me I was at least awake
The many evenings when I could not think
But sat enjoying my pulse till daybreak

Turning the chained and fated pages
Was like fumbling with soft life
Melted years mouthed into the ocean
Of pages clouded and wet with tears

But one more page—tomorrow's page
Misty like a reflecting mirror
Showing the shimmering wrinkles of age
And the trenched islands of horror.

The time when sensation goes out of my fingertips
I must distinguish hot and cold by instinct
The time when I must know myself Controller of events
Which have been governed only by the sense

What if I am a recessive mutation
Destined to give way in time
To the surge of biological motion
Which raised the mammal from the reptile?

Then the candle grease and ink
Insomnia and drink

Would be just another link
When I have gone over the brink.

Elegy of Midnight

L. S. Senghor

Summer splendid Summer, feeding the Poet with the milk of
your light
I grew like corn in the Springtime, I was drunk with verdure
of water, with green rustling in the gold of Time
Ah! no longer! I cannot bear your light, the light of your
lamps, your atomic light breaking up all my being
I cannot bear the light of midnight. The splendour of honours
is like a Sahara
An immense void, without erg or hamada without grass, without
the flicker of an eyelash, or the flicker of a heart.
So twenty-four hours out of twenty-four, eyes wide open like
Father Cloarec
Crucified on the stone by the Heathens of Joal, worshippers of
Serpents.
In my eyes the Portuguese lighthouse turned, yes twenty-four
hours out of twenty-four
A machine precise and unrelenting until the end of time.

I leap out of my bed, a leopard in the snare. A sudden gust of
Simoon sands up my throat.
Ah! if I could crumple into the dung and blood, into the void.
I pace among my books. They gaze at me from the bottoms
of their eyes
Six thousand lamps burning twenty-four hours out of twenty-
four.
I am standing up, strangely lucid
And I am handsome as the hundred yards runner, as the black
Mauretanian stallion in rut.
I wash down in my blood a river of seed to make fertile all
Byzantine plains
And the hills, the austere hills.
I am the Lover and the locomotive with well-oiled piston.

Sweetness of her lips being strawberries, denseness of her body
    being stone, sweetness of her secret being peach
Her body, deep earth laid open to the black Sower.
The Spirit springs under the groin, in the matrix of desire
The sex an antenna at the centre of the Many, exchanges
    fulgurant messages.
I can no longer find peace in the music of love, in the sacred
    rhythms of the poem.
Against despair O Lord, I have need of all my strength
—Sweetness of the dagger full in the heart up to the hilt
Like remorse. I am not sure to die.
If that was Hell, the absence of sleep, the desert of the Poet
The pain of living, dying of not dying
The agony of darkness, that passion of death and light
Like moths at night round the storm lamps in the horrible rot
    of a virgin forest.

Lord of the light and the darkness
Thou Lord of the Cosmos let me rest under the shade of Joal
Let me be born again into the Kingdom of Childhood alive with
    rustling dreams
Let me be the shepherd to my shepherdess among the sea-flats
    of Dyilor where the dead prosper .
Let me burst into clapping when Tening-N'dyare and
    Tyagum-N'dyare enter the circle
Let me dance like the Athlete to the drum of the year's Dead.
All this is only a prayer. You know my peasant patience.
Peace will come, the Angel of Dawn will come, the song of the
    preposterous birds will come
The light of dawn will come
I shall sleep the sleep of death by which the Poet is fed
(O Thou who givest sleeping sickness to newborn babies, to
    Marone the Poetess, to Kotye-Barma the Just!)
I shall sleep at dawn, my pink doll in my arms
My doll with green eyes and golden, and so wonderful a tongue
Being the tongue of the poem.

Ulysses

Notes from here to my Joyce class

Wole Soyinka

Haunting the music of the mind, I watched
Once, through sun slats, a raindrop
Lengthen out to rivers on a window-pane
And on this painless rack of time, stretched
I was, heritage of thought, clay and voices
Passing easily to wind and rain-becoming
And, lest I lose the landmarks of my being
Pocked the air with terse, echoing rounds
Drumtap feelers on the growth of leaves.

This storm has cold wings, and they beat
An interchange in time to death and birth
The rain's harrowing passion, midwife love
Winds newcomer-wanderer in its toils.
Lodged in barrenness of ante-rooms
To manger-haven, I, sleep-walker through
The weary cycle of the season's womb
Labouring to give birth to her deathless self,
One more reveller at the rites, I watch
The years re-lay their yeasting dregs
Beneath the froth, hard soles travel pressed
In poultice of new loam. We embrace,
The world and I in great infinitudes.
I grow into that portion of the world
Lapping my feet, yet bear the rain of nails
That drill within to the archetypal heart
Of all lone wanderers.

How pleasant to have toyed with concepts.
Time—we touched upon it—Time I hold
Beyond my hands, a febrile heart slowing
To the calm of death. It weighs all and nothing,
Ceased with rain and ran between my fingers.
It was a crystal cover on the world

A rake of thunders showered its fragments
To a slow dissolve in hailstones, and I was
Held awhile to its truthfulness of transience.
But not for long. It flowed to raise a flotsam from
Tobacco shreds, weaving space inflated
To a swell of dancing seas and pygmy fountains—
Detritus of change, warts on continuity
Drowned steeples of the broken sees, tossed thorn
In matriseas—mud consummation. I trail
A sea-weed cord to hold your breaths to mine
Prime turd among a sea of faeces—oh how
We surf-wrestle to manure the land at ebb!
How golden finally is the recovered fleece?
A question we refuse to ask the Bard.

It turns on quest cycles, to track a skein
Of self through eyeless veils, stumble on warps
Endure the blinds of spidery distortions, till
Swine-scented folds and caressing tunnels
Come to crossroads at the straits, between
Vaginal rocks. Here, the moment of time's
Overlap, forfeiture of flesh, we shed
Our questions, here, turn from bridging
Passes of eroded runs, from scratching
Upon the calloused skin of blind redemptive
Doors. On minds grown hoary from the quest
Rest, rooted even in the turmoil agency
A boulder solitude amidst wine-centred waves
And hold, in paradox of lighthouse windows
On dark-fallen seas, our lighted beings
Suspended as mirages on the world's reality.

Communion *Tchicaya U Tam'si*

When man is more loyal to man
woman more heedful of the moon
the child gentle under his father's touch
my hands tracing a dawn
life will reinvent my body
my memory suddenly made flint
no longer mould the clay of crime
on the back of any brother of mine

O light of the Last Supper's bread!
O warmth of wine in that cup!
all in the image of a blessed womb!
already my life has stopped devouring me . . .

Once it was sad to be a man
each colour of the body was a ghetto
no way out through the pores but sweat
wherever I was shadow the whip cracked
but now it is my tongue I crack
at the sweet taste that now the nettle has
since I learnt to make my voice a balm

Matting to Weave *Tchicaya U Tam'si*

He had given away the secret of the sun
now he would write the poem of his life

why are there crystals in his blood
why are there corpuscles in his laughter

his soul had ripened
then someone called him
dirty nigger head

now he is left with the gentleness of his laughter
and the giant tree of that sharp laceration

what was the land where as a deer he dwells
behind the deer before behind the deer

his river was the firmest dish
being made of bronze
being his living flesh

it was then he told himself
no my life is not a poem

here is the tree the water and the stones
and then this priesthood of perpetual change

better enjoy your wine
get up early in the mornings
they told him

but no more birds within the mother's loving care

dirty nigger head
he is the younger brother of fire

here the bush begins
and the sea is only a memory of gulls
all ranged erect teeth to teeth
against the foam of a cardinal dance

the tree was thickest set with leaves
the bark of the tree was tenderest—

after the bush is burnt what more to say

why was there absinthe in the wine
why restore to the hearts
the caymans and the canoe-men
and the river wave

a grain of sand between the teeth
is this the way the world is ground
no

no
his river was the gentlest dish
the firmest
it was his most living flesh

here the poem of his life begins
he was dragged to school
he was dragged to a factory
and saw his way down avenues of sphinxes

now he is left with the gentle arc of his laughter
and the tree and the water and the leaves

this is why as you will see
canoe-men on foot have taken up once more
from the French cotton tug-boats
their clamorous cries

this flight is a flight of doves

    the leeches did not know the bitterness
    of such blood
    in the most hygienic dish

    dirty nigger head
    here is my Congo head

    the most hygienic dish

Having found no men
on my horizon
with my body I played
the blazing poem of death
I followed my river
to the strong cold surges
I was open to the world
of sea-weed
where solitudes swarm
To solitudes open the thickets
To the sun
open my flesh
To ripe blood rebellions
real semen draws me breath by breath
into the yeast of leaves and hurricanes

my hair rough to all the winds
buttresses
my hands damp to all the seeds
carry my feet deep into all regions
into all regions
slow death absorbs me with his plutocratic suns

false presence
I will be treacherous
and then god of hosts
christ has betrayed me
by letting them spike his skin
he wanted them to put him to the test of death

traitor christ
here is my flesh turned bronze
and my blood clenched
by my innumerable selves copper and zinc
by the two stones of my brain
everlasting by my slow death
coelacanth

a scent of vervain and of deer
torments me and I hear voices welling tardy
in the day
the day passes the zenith
with a learned procession of cicadas
if I thought of my own good it is time to say goodbye
yet no I have still got a job to do

High above the Madaraka crowds
the flywhisk leaps
towards the sun
at the first splatter of drums
and remains poised,

White mane thrown back
cocking its head
listening.

Drumsticks rain upon membranes,
throat fibres arc
and send bushfires thro' brass-
bulges and trampolines
take up the uproar
the flywhisk remains poised.

Flags lacerate the equatorial sky
urged on by a timely wind
that senses it is time
for song of the land
the flywhisk remains poised,

Proclaiming its point,
the spire must outlast the length of the song,
the strained duration of military fingertips
that lean towards foreheads of warriors,
the flywhisk remains poised.

The effort within the civilian spine
leans against the extended pillar,
a chorus to the proclamation
the flywhisk remains poised.

The rhythm subsides, the wind wipes it,
liberated palms plunge earthward furling,

the joints of a crowd collapse on the incline,
momentarily, in excellency of stance,
the flywhisk remains poised.

My Mother Who Art ...   *Jared Angira*

Accept me on your laps
And let me close your womb
The fortune of your birthhood

Teeth are but bones
Laughing at the lame

Let me laugh
With the happy robins
The child who closed your uterus
Leaving its walls embracing

Middle-borns do not sweat
The pain of opening the tunnel
And me
The weight of slamming the cavestone

Civilization born
Of unvirgin lands
So wave the flag
And let me hear your maiden voice

Tears are but expressions
Of selected feelings

Let me suckle your breasts
Before they become
Mere antiques of human history
No poison shall pass
No one trails by
Miracles have ceased

For dreams are but pictures
Of the foetal empire.

Rosbella Adhiambo   *Jared Angira*

I feel the presence of that rugged woman
Whose shadow stands untrammelled

The cinders of joy have billowed seawards
Beyond the hanging sky

She has nothing to do
With this exotic desert

The logics of existence
Have damned her solo voice

She floated the deep seas
In stormy days, passed the reefs

She was alone on the Flood Day
Swept to the lee, with discarded leaves
Of the dismembered life of conjugant toys

She held her shoulders
To the earth's foundation

The years have put some deeper paint
On the statue, O Time, that once was fair

I feel the touch of her fingers
Striking the lead fibres of my harp

The house whose outer wall
Suffers the weather's wrath
And stands in the centre of the city.

The value shoots up, the house still stands
Antique to memory, valuable to present

The touch of the holy water
The pond they polluted

The inner wall of that woman
Stands untouched by those fouled hands.

His Excellency the Masquerader

J. P. Clark

He serves
To ford between swamp and sand,
He serves!

The bridge stands,
All that stone and steel put together,
It stands;

But bolts drop,
And steel that should be blue
At close grip

Shows brown . . .
And for such service, songs more than
Water and sand:

In Ojoto
So they worship the masks,
Altho' in season—

The masks!
O take off the mask! And behind?
What wind! What straw!

Agbor Dancer   *J. P. Clark*

See her caught in the throb of a drum
Tippling from hide-brimmed stem
Down lineal veins to ancestral core
Opening out in her supple tan
Limbs like fresh foliage in the sun.

See how entangled in the magic
Maze of music
In trance she treads the intricate
Pattern rippling crest after crest
To meet the green clouds of the forest.

Tremulous beats wake trenchant
In her heart a descant
Tingling quick to her finger tips
And toes virginal habits long
Too atrophied for pen or tongue.

Could I, early sequester'd from my tribe,
Free a lead-tether'd scribe
I should answer her communal call
Lose myself in her warm caress
Intervolving earth, sky and flesh.

Foreboding   *Ismael Hurreh*

Solo:
My brother you sealed on us your sighs of hypocrisy
My brother with magnetic eyes for these cactus faces on us
And for these wrinkles of contempt on the face of Somalia
We will chant you necklaces of dry bones:

Chorus:
What we are (we should have said)
Are empty voices in the dark

Emptier than our chants in crises
What we are (we should have said)
Are dangerous rats scuttling in dry paths.

Solo:

My sophisticated brother with mountains of kinsmen's power
Our gory spears awaiting spears of other tribesmen
Arrayed with blue loincloth and white star-shaped shields
We will chant you hymns chanted to Sheikh Abdulkadir
Mourning the death of corn fields at your hands
Your hands sublimer than distant clouds
When dry mouths gape and drop dead of thirst.

Chorus:

Do you not hear these blind drums in our voices?
Do you not see us prostrating with blind hearts?
Do you not find us cold-blooded?
Do you not fear us causing plagues?

Solo:

And at the onset of pain pangs of Africa's birth
We have heard you fluting ominous tales
Behind bank doors barred to us
We have heard you counting biles and eyes

Of dead bats and mouths drivelling your praises
And soon we will see you dismantling our kidneys
In parlours for diplomats
And in conjugal parties.

Martin Luther King   *Amin Kassam*

under abraham's vacant eyes
he proclaimed a dream
a dream
that blossomed a sun
where darkness had reigned

a dream
that bestrode the eagle
with ringing heart
wheeling high above
flailing truncheons thudding
on bare flesh
from rocky desert
he carved a green valley
where soil and clouds
embraced and fused
with the voice of man
tearing into his neck . . .

To the Soldier Hero
Mazisi Kunene

Who was Langula
That he should trample over a thousand victims
And praise himself over their graves?
Is it not true: for him there was only one great joy—
To hold the iron dripping with their blood,
As though this fame
Fulfils all life's ambition?
But even he who sharpened the edge of hearts
Conceived new truths,
Telling us that truth is not the truth of swords,
But the long buds growing from the ruins.

Just a Passerby
Oswald Mbuyiseni Mtshali

I saw them clobber him with kieries,
I heard him scream with pain
like a victim of slaughter;
I smelt fresh blood gush
from his nostrils,
and flow on the street.

I walked into the church,
and knelt in the pew
"Lord! I love you,
I also love my neighbour. Amen."

I came out
my heart as light as an angel's kiss
on the cheek of a saintly soul.

Back home I strutted
past a crowd of onlookers.
Then she came in—
my woman neighbour:
"Have you heard? They've killed your brother."
"O! No! I heard nothing. I've been to church."

The Birth of Shaka
Oswald Mbuyiseni Mtshali

His baby cry
was of a cub
tearing the neck
of the lioness
because he was fatherless.

The gods
boiled his blood
in a clay pot of passion
to course in his veins.

His heart was shaped into an ox shield
to foil every foe.

Ancestors forged
his muscles into
thongs as tough
as wattle bark

and nerves
as sharp as
syringa thorns.

His eyes were lanterns
that shone from the dark valleys of Zululand
to see white swallows
coming across the sea.
His cry to two assassin brothers:

"Lo! you can kill me
but you'll never rule this land!"

Introduction

Richard Ntiru

Perhaps it was his Ugil shirt—
The missing button
The unassertive collar;
Perhaps it was his knotty hair,
That boasted little acquaintance with the comb;
Or maybe it was his usualness
 —One more impersonal handshake
Along the constant street—
That induced the functional smile
And operated the mechanical handshake.

His name didn't help either:
Mugabo Mugenge—You'd heard the name
In the Out-patients' attendance queue;
Not in the current Telephone Directory!

You certainly needed prompting.
I said he was an old-time friend
But you continued to wave to passing cars;
I added that he was a high placed man
And you promptly took your cue
 —"A University teacher, author of several works"—

"Re-e-e-ally? Er-Um-oh! . . ."
And you became word and emotion perfect.
Like a dog that mistakes thief for visitor
And remembers to bark at his master's coughing,
You renewed and pumped the handshake
—Reshaped your mouth to a proper smile
—Recalled his famous public talk
That you had regretfully missed . . .
And observed, thoughtfully,
How unlike his photographs he looked.

You were tuned—
Delved deep into his latest novel
And wondered why his main characters
Do not walk on the solid earth
And fail to effect living communication.
You'd have rambled on, no longer looking at him,
But he quipped:
"They are in good company."
And was about to add, when you knowledgeably interrupted,
"Society is a market stall
And men goods on display
Where the label is more important than the labelled
And the price more fascinating than the value."

We parted, hoping to meet again.
You went away rehearsing his name
But probably unremembering his face.

The Prodigals

Odia Ofeimun

We scan the putrid initials
of yesterpalmwine on the faceless saunter
of these prodigals. Grim shadows
astride the malformed limbs of a truth.
Along the parapet of hypocrisy,

they throng, reek of the grime
of, yet to be, decoded days.

This dusk, they juju their ways
downhill: loud medals of our sorry tale.
Their heads are claimed by clouds.
Their eyes recede from tomorrow.
No sense of mission sustains them.

The arid argument of their bootsteps
on the tarmac suggests
a need to give the foul, depraved past
a hood of royal beads.

For Christopher Okigbo

Odia Ofeimun

The drum is silenced in mid-throb;
the fiute is flung away;
and ears strain to master the malediction
of the thunder;

And the gongbells acquiesce
abandoned now, to the cobwebbed bleakness,
the scab-clotted corner of
the sacrificial groove

For, the air is lost
to the teething missive of the sifting earth
Even the earth itself is lost
And the laughter of cannon, of thunder,
arraigns the multitude of wills
in savage tutelage

And the drum is silenced in mid-throb

And charged,
beyond arms' reach
beyond the power of our ululations to recall

you brandish your unripened selves—
riddles, in the galloping peals of this
derailed sun

Through the labyrinth of a thankless
Nirvana
you ride on the back of your white elephant
into the Deep Cloud

Lost Friends
Lenrie Peters

They are imprisoned
In dark suits and air-conditioned offices
Alsatians ready at the door
On the saliva carpeted floor

They spend their nights
In jet airlines—
Would change them in mid-air
To show how much they dare

Drunk from the vertigo
Of never catching their tails
They never seem to know
When not to bite their nails

Their new addiction
Fortifies their livers
They are getting there
While the going's good
They have no time for dreamers.

Fado Singer
for Amalia Roderiguez

My skin is pumiced to a fault
I am down to hair-roots, down to fibre filters
Of the raw tobacco nerve

Your net is spun of sitar strings
To hold the griefs of gods: I wander long
In tear vaults of the sublime

Queen of night torments, you strain
Sutures of song to bear imposition of the rites
Of living and of death. You

Pluck strange dirges from the storm
Sift rare stones from ashes of the moon, and rise
Night errands to the throne of anguish

Oh there is too much crush of petals
For perfume, too heavy tread of air on mothwing
For a cup of rainbow dust

Too much pain, oh midwife at the cry
Of severance, fingers at the cosmic cord, too vast
The pains of easters for a hint of the eternal.

I would be free of your tyranny, free
From sudden plunges of the flesh in earthquake
Beyond all subsidence of sense

I would be free from headlong rides
In rock seams and volcanic veins, drawn   dark steeds
On grey melodic reins.

Eye of a calf
Neck like the crested crane's
Legs like young banana stems
Gums bright as a babe's
Teeth that out-glitter ice
Foot delicate as a child's
O eyes of the calf, O child-voice,
O heart-drum—let me die with you.

Ndela, Son of Sompisi
Traditional (from the Zulu)

Rattler of spears!
He who is unable to lie down, one side being red with wounds,
He whose wounds are as numerous as the huts of a large kraal.
Hornbill that is reluctant to set out,
Long-tailed leaper like a leopard,
Redbuck that escapes again and again.
Daily they stab the Rattler but he retaliates;
How many of them come back again?
Who come back again when a person acts so deliberately?
He who crosses over to the other side,
Who crosses and the whole Ntolela regiment crosses,
Stout stick that points to the Ngwane people
He who attacks people with fury, he of the Rattlers.
> At day-break Ndela was left
> When the army returned,
> At dawn Ndela remained,
> Feeble I remain behind,
> Paltry strength equal to that of a child.
Body of which the Nkayiya regiment sits,
The Nkayiyas of Swide,
He who is always wounded in the face like a prince
Great branch, turn back the Ntolela regiment;
News that came first to Shaka at the Mbelebele kraal.
Have you a piece of gut long enough

To sew up Ndela's wounds?
He who crosses over to the other side,
He who is embroiled across the Thukela.

Traditional (from the Swahili)

O tapster of soured wine, from the sheath of the withered palm
Draw wine for me in the pipkin-jar that was tapped by my
    own tapster.
Draw wine for me in the little flask that makes a man stagger
    and sway.
Draw wine for me in wine-jar hot-mulled and dregged of its lees.
When I am well wined I stand demanding my keen-edged
    sword,
My keen-edged sword with its guard-leaves of steel and its hilt
    of mtupa wood.
My keen-edged sword that hangs from the peg where the war-
    horn and trumpets hang.
Where are slung the state-drums and the rack-edged spears of
    battle.

Traditional (from the Bakiga)

Sorghum, sorghum, O sorghum,
Sorghum, and Kiga are one
When you have a guest
You give him sorghum beer.

Through the upturned soil
Two shoots first show themselves.
During the rains
The tiny plant begins to swell and tremble,
More shoots emerge
To peer at sun and moon.

The farmer keenly watches
This life plant, mother of people

From whose juice grows the black blood
That nourishes young and old.

As the rains endure, and weeds multiply,
He must clean his plot,
Toiling through torrents,
Resting only in the torrid night
Till the plant begins to flower
And a crown of berries, green-shining to copper,
Is its spear-head
Over grass and pollen grain.
The season's march brings birds,
Many birds. They soar, dive, perch and peck.
They plunder the lovely sorghum fruit.
They sing in discords and in chorus.
O "happy season of harvest time":
Cuckoos, weavers, crows and partridges—
They fly, they mate, they feed
O merry time, O sorghum!

Then with his curved knife
Singing and whistling among the stalks
The farmer fells the sorghum
Jolly fat women chop off the berry
Youths carry it home.
When the brew is ready
Men suck through tubes the juice
They sing, shout, groan and howl,
They stoop, dance, and lie down,
They fall under the heavy potent weight.
Who cares? "Tis harvest time,"
Sing women in the inner room
Dancing in praise.

To Palm Wine   *Traditional (from the Yoruba)*

Alimotu of the gourd
Lamihun in the fibrous clump
Dawn it is that heralds your approach
When evening comes, the drum crooks taps
Taps, taps in gladness
Mistress of tuppence only, yet
Chased the millionaire into the forest.

You are that which the horse drank
Drank, drank and forgot his horns
You are that which the cock drank
Drank, drank, and forgot to urinate
You are that which the guinea-fowl drank
Drank, till a cry pierced his throat
And he took to the wilds . . .

Traditional (from the Swahili)

Praise my bow with haft of the wild-vine, let it be dressed with
    oil and shine like glass
When I set out I shot a snake through its throat and I shot an
    elephant through its ear as it trumpeted
Then I shot a piebald crow and a duiker running away and they
    tell me,
Stand aside, son of Mbwasho, lay your weapons aside.

Music Maker   *Kalu Uka*

i orchestrate the silver in a rain-
drop and the dust in a faded star;
they, in muscular meandering dive with
this current's backwash beneath arch-
ed highways shut from rain and clouds.

callisthenically my music rises to meet
its dancers—burgeoning god-deniers
and desert-rock affirmers and wisely
indifferent ignoramuses who see but paradigms;
my music bears the mystic light to incense.

The dancers and me fuse our syncopated
rhythms in open dance, right feet first;
then dream and sail the waters round us—
callisthenically rising to meet the swell
on starved ankles, the bulge on empty stomachs.

XVIII
Prayers, Invocations

Were I Clever

Were I clever
I'd send me back
to mother's womb
and build me new
tough placenta
and feed me more
on foetal food.

Were I clever
I'd send me back
to mother's womb
and lay in ambush
for an ideal day
when laughter is the houseboy
and tears
mere hearsay.

Were I clever
I'd court me
an osaye princess
and dwell us there
where rainbow is the estate
and love the landlord.

Were I clever
I'd build me mansions
on the grassless sky
and install me music
platonic
and plant me choir
of parrots and pigeons
and excel the same
Oh were I clever!

The Harvest of Our Life

Kwesi Brew

If this is the time
To master my heart
Do so!
Do so now!
As the clouds float
Home to their rain-drenched
Caverns behind the hills.

If this is the time
To master my heart,
Let me fall an easy victim
To the pleasures that you hold to my lips
When the duiker
Lingers along the pool to drink
And the ailing leopard
Turns its dry unbelieving snout away;
When the dew-drops dry
Unnoticed on the sinews of the leaf
And the soft-paddling duck
Webs its way
Through the subtle
Entanglement of weeds,
Along the river Prah.

Oh, I remember the songs
You sang that night,
And the whirl of raffia skirts;
The speechless pulsations of living bones.
Oh I remember the songs you sang
Recounting what has gone before
And what is ours beyond
The tracks of our thoughts and feet

You sang of beautiful women
(The kangaroo-jumps of their youthful breasts)
Flirting with sportive spirits

Red-eyed, with red-lips, hoary-red
With quaffing of frequent libations;
You sang of feasts and festivals;
The red blood-line across the necks
Of sacrificial sheep;
Of acceptance and refusal of gifts;
Of sacrifices offered and withheld;
Of good men and their lot;
Of good name and its loss; of the die cast
And the loading of the dice;
Why the barndog barked
At the moon as she sang
And why the mouse dropped the pearl-corn
From its teeth and stood forced-humble
With the soft light of fear in its eyes.

I saw a sheen of light
On the soft belly of the leaves
Dream-worn in the night
Bright as the light
Defending day from night
And palm-wine as clear
As the path of a spirit as water,
And her hair like the dark eyes of an eagle
Over the affairs of men.

And yet the river rolled on
And passed over rocks;
White sand in the bed
Bearing the burden of rotten wood
Twigs, grass—a flower—the breath
Of the soil and the bones of thousands
Who should have lived
To fight a war for this or that
And this or that a ruse
To deceive the mover of the move
And the mover of the move
Always moved by an uncertainty.

And yet to fight
And yet to conquer:
This was the badge we bore
On the pale texture of our hearts.
And yet to fight
And yet to conquer.
The sea-gulls blow
Like paper-pieces over the hard blue sea
And yet we live to conquer.
So we talked of wards
With their women
And they wept at the foot of the hills.

And the waters rolled on.
And what was old was new
And what was new never came to stay.
But to skim the gates of change;
Forever new; forever old and new;
Once-upon-a-time,
Never the same,
Always at last the same.
And her hair was dark and her pride undimmed
By the dusty struggles
Of strong men over her shadow
And yet the river rolled on.
And the river rolled on.

Her thighs slipped-slipped
Through the folds of her cloth
As always, once-upon-a-time.
But those who slept with her in those mud huts
(Arrows in their grips
And bows on their shoulders)
Have crawled away soft-bellied,
Into hollow chambers
Along the road;
Lined their walls
With smooth white stones;

Abandoned the shade
That sheltered their peace
And call that peace of mind
Now floating away with the clouds
As peace—
That passes understand

If this is the time
To master our hearts
Do so!
Do so now!

Pardon Me

Ismael Hurren

pardon me father if I am a disappointment to what you
expect of me

                              pardon me father

if I cannot slaughter other tribesmen
if I do not say my prayers in the morning
if I turn my back on some of your advice

                              because father

although your blood runs in my veins
although I too have been a nomad
although I've slept under roofless huts

                              eyeing the moon

and raising my hands to God
and envying His might
time has unfolded many strange sheets
and spread them between us
time has uprooted me
time has transplanted me to grounds
where prayer is of no use,

and mother pardon me for digging your bones out
(your bones that were buried here)

if I had forgotten that you were buried here.

Grass Will Grow   *Jonathan Kariar*

If you should take my child Lord
Give my hands strength to dig his grave
Cover him with earth
Lord send a little rain
For grass will grow.

If my house should burn down
So that the ashes sting the nostrils
Making the eyes weep
Then Lord send a little rain
For grass will grow.

But Lord do not send me
Madness
I ask for tears
Do not send me moon-hard madness
To lodge snug in my skull
I would you sent me hordes of horses
'Galloping
Crushing
But do not break
The yolk of the moon on me.

The Desert

Amin Kassam

hear my burning cry o heavens!
hear the lament
of a disillusioned soul
whose footprints weave drunkenly
across the desert floor
you have seen me trudging
across the sands
through whirling storms
staggering over dunes
gasping with thirst
you have seen my steps falter
in oozing sand
you have seen me crawl towards
dry scintillant water
and yet beneath your relentless gaze
i still plead,
plead for but a drop!

even the cactus raises hinged arms
aloft in supplication.
is there no emotion in you o heavens,
no compassion
must i believe we are robots,
that the spark of humanity is lost
then i am not alone
for many have crossed this floor
many have looked to the garden
with hopeful despair
as though at a mirage
and wept
hear my whisper o heavens
before i fall
i have not the strength
to thunder forth my words
in this land ravaged of hope

where bleached bones
seem to say
despair of escape ...
perhaps there is no return.

Redemption

Frank Kobina Parkes

My world pines in your marble breasts, daughter of woe
Green buds crack in the dry harmattan wind
Sun beats down on the city of a million dead
Men wove hats with their hands for a shelter
And monkeys, from tree-tops bare, mock
With crown-capped glee
Bare-headed among the despoiled flowers I stand
Empty-handed, in built-up deserts
I groan mankind's loss
And search wide heavens for a sign not written there

I am a stranger ...

My mother's house is desolate and bare
I, stranger upon earth, walk alone the misty pavements
Where bright sun shines and brings no warmth
As snowflakes parachute to rescue earth

Yet you are shivering, daughter of the land

I feel, can touch and yearn to chant old psalms
Recorded on soundtracks through Adam's mind
But I am no more human
Purged of mankind-knowing griefs
Snobbery passes me by
And I have lost my voice
In the whining of the arctic winds bleak and sharp
Despair withdraws from my cold paw in friendship shot
Alone. I prowl, being with soul lone as a star
That twinkles in a firmament of crushed-out eyes

Depths are frozen wombs
Barren skulls and cross-bones picked
And earth belongs to other races—-pressed in steel

I am lost . . . and you . . .
And what shall we make
Of all these shining orbs and incandescent tombs?

The sun is dark, is cold the sun
I am a potter's vessel shaped by knowing hands
Fallen from sky of earth-dreams that never flower
The eye of the Lord is on me
(and His wrath too)
How long,
How long shall I riddle rock breasts for warmth
How long shall I, a worn Silesian exile, turn
Sore feet for refuge to shrines of past oppression?

Suffer me
O suffer me not to be separated
Firm breasts that milked my toothless gum

In the desert place
Let my cry come unto Thee!

I shall return
I shall return to sun-warmed lands
Where rivers flow all through the year
I shall return with the glory of sun-down
Only to battered citadels will I return
To washed-in skulls and sun-picked bones
Wild groans of shattered hearthstones pierce my ears
Knock, O knock down the battlements of pride

Caress stone breasts with benumbed hands
That fire may rise
And coldness burn
And warmth return

And in red glow, behold
That sign sure writ in blood
Shall these bones live?
Shall these bones live?

The streams of Life gush out in tuneful song
Dead bones in rocky caves astir
Dead bones in mansions moving,
As the glory of God descends on earth

To be despoiled.

At a Thrift-Club Feast   *Traditional (from the Yoruba)*

All you persons of prestige here gathered together,
I greet the woodcock with its characteristic "mese" cry.
I cannot help talking, Man-of-many-styles, the Gaboon viper
    attacks with its mouth.
The belly's mark on the ground betrays the path taken by a
    snake along a farm-plot boundary!
As all you members of the club are met here today,
Complete in number as the coins paid for tax by a citizen,
Death shall not cut your hearts across like the nodes of tuberous
    yams.
Numerous as you are, like brown ants,
Ogun shall not let death cut your hearts across like the nodes
    of tuberous yams.
We shall for very long enjoy each other's company.
Every fifth day, kolanuts are seen set out for sale on raffia trays.
White star-apples naturally appear on the ground in increasing
    numbers.
We shall be coming here.
You we shall be seeing here.
Your place shall never be filled by a stranger.
The bottle-gourd warps its own fruit, not the fruit of another
    plant.

People who beat the drum of wickedness desire that it should sound forth.

God shall prevent its sounding forth.

If an elder beats the drum of wickedness and it sounds forth

Only his children will dance to the music.

He who scoops up water from a pool pulls down the fishes' abode, damages the fishes' abode.

He who hoes up a weedy plot of land damages the bushfowl's abode.

With a short club or truncheon we reduce mud walls' broken pieces to powdery clay.

A house of his is being built on earth

And a house of his is being built in heaven.

He said: "Let us with a sacrifice break down the house in heaven

And rebuild the one on earth."

Then the elders of heaven put their mighty heads together.

The result was: "Rats are beaten with rods, birds are beaten with rods.

Cloths are beaten with rods, hides and skins are beaten with rods.

With a flat-faced mallet, the earth is beaten flat."

If any man is seeking your hurt, all you people here,

His skull shall become an oval-shaped drinking-vessel,

Only once does the *èbùré* vegetable bear fruits and then it perishes.

And my mother, Osorounga, who kills people but gets nothing of their legacy,

Who attacks at night.

If she's seeking your hurt, all you people here,

Her skull shall become an oval-shaped drinking-vessel.

Only once does the *èbùré* vegetable bear fruits and then it perishes.

Now I say, "All to no purpose is the rumbling among the tree-top coconuts.

All to no purpose is the rumbling among the elephant-grass bushes.

All to no purpose, all to no purpose is the mound-making done
    by swarming brown ants.

The two hundred flies that have clung to a horse's tail the horse
    smashes to death with his tail."

This was the pronouncement of the Ifa oracle to Arilegbe of
    heaven,

Who pushed over walls of ruin to defeat his enemies.

I have pushed over walls of ruins to defeat Orotimi, all you my
    colleagues here gathered together.

Likewise, every one of you should push over walls of ruins to
    defeat your enemy.

This is my conclusion, you inmates here.

Let none of you complain of not knowing how I finished my
    chant,

I the rascally child, a die-hard like a civet-cat, a person
    associated with the buffalo

Which carries an òrìṣà's emblem on its head.

Incantation to Gain Popularity   *Traditional (from the Yoruba)*

You cannot dispute the forest with a rat.
You cannot dispute the savannah with the buffalo.
You cannot dispute his father's title with Olukere.
    You cannot play with a snake.
    You cannot dance with a praying mantis.
A small child cannot beat his mother.
An old man cannot get annoyed with his own shit.
A woman cannot look at the penis—without being glad
Look at me then, and be glad!
    The children are enjoying themselves with the birds.
    Children of the house, elders of the house,
    Men, women, young and old,
You cannot see a new born babe—without happiness.
    I am now a new born babe;
    Come and dance with me.

XIX
Miscellany

Fashion

Amin Kassam

phone dangling,
from my ear, two
one on each side
three, red, bouncing in the air
like those i saw
in an office yesterday

only, they were on a desk

crispness of reply shows
authority and power
which i feel
when i hold a clenched fist
to my cheek
and adjust it to bring
the mouth-piece about an inch
under my chin

i am ready
shall we use the script

To a Bed-Bug

Sam Mbure

I wonder how long, you awful parasite,
Shall share with me this little bed,
And make me, from my sweet dreams be lost,
By sucking blood from my poor head.

I should but say man has much
Blood, which you and your families do feed
On; for supper, dinner, and lunch,
And besides, you do in my bed breed.

Clever thou art, tiny creature;
You attend me when I am deep asleep;
When thou art sure, I can't you capture,
Just at the time I snore deep.

'Tis so strange that before twilight,
The bed clear of you would seem;
For not one of you is in my sight;
As if your presence was in a dream.

The Miniskirt   *Richard Ntiru*

To visualize what you can't see:
That's the paradoxical pleasure of the mind.

In the afterbirth of seeing,
Death of imagination.

To dally on the brink of reality:
That's the snug illusion of life.

In the capitulation of the summit,
Paradoxical disappointment.

Now is the legend beyond
Become the cliché of the elements.

Shall the synthetic gauze
Atone for the beauty of the fertility lines?

Landing on the Moon   *Odia Ofeimun*

Gobble the news with seven grains
of alligator pepper, a pinch of salt,
white chalk, one sea-deep cry
for man's hike to Jehovah-hood, or,
must we not submerge in rituals
this explosive moment of animal triumph?—
Catch my hand, brother
we are annexing the kingdom of the gods.

Index of Poets and Poems

352

354

Biographical Notes

Biographical Notes

Abangira   Student at the University of Nairobi. Published in *Dhana*.

G. Adali-Mortty — Born in Northern Eweland, Ghana, and educated at Achimota and Cornell University. He has worked as a teacher, social worker, adult educationalist and administrator, and is now Lecturer in Business Management in the University of Ghana. Published in *Okyeame*, etc.

Costa Andrade   Born in Lepi, Angola, in 1936. As a student in Lisbon he was active in the Cultural Movement of the Casa dos Estudantes do Imperio. Publications: *Terra de Acacias Rubras, Tempo Angolano na Italia.*

Jared Angira   Born in Kenya. He studied commerce at the University of Nairobi where he was editor of *Busara.* He is Africa's representative on the International Executive Committee of the World University Service, and was a founder, and is treasurer, of the Writers' Association of Kenya. He now works for the East African Harbours Corporation in Dar es Salaam. Collections: *Juices, Silent Voices.*

Peter Anyang'-Nyong'O   Born in Uganda, and educated at Ndiru and Makerere University. Scriptwriter and broadcaster for the Schools Broadcasting Division of the Voice of Kenya from 1965, he is now in the Department of Political Science of the University of Chicago.

Kofi Awoonor   Born at Wheta, Ghana. Formerly Director of the Ghana Film Corporation, he is now Visiting Professor in African Literature at the State University of New York at Stony Brook. Novel: *This Earth My Brother*; collections: *Rediscovery, Night of my Blood.*

Kwesi Brew   Born in 1928 at Cape Coast, Ghana, and educated at the University of Ghana. A diplomat, he served in India and West Germany before becoming Ghana's first Ambassador to Mexico. He is now Ambassador to Senegal. Collection: *Shadows of Laughter.*

Dennis Brutus   Born in 1924 in Salisbury, Southern Rhodesia, and educated at Fort Hare and the University of the Witwatersrand. Political campaigns against apartheid led to house-arrest and then to a sentence of eighteen months' hard labour. He emigrated from South Africa in 1966 and is now Professor of English at Northwestern University in Illinois. He is Acting Chairman of the International Campaign Against Racism in Sport, and the UN Representative for International Defence and Aid. Collections: *Sirens Knuckles Boots, Letters to Martha, Poems from Algiers* and *Thoughts Abroad*, all included in

A Simple Lust; numerous critical articles and poems in *Transition*, *Black Orpheus*, etc.

Siriman Cissoko   Born in Mali, resident in Senegal. Published in *Présence Africaine*, etc.

J. P. Clark   Born in 1935 in the Ijaw country of the Niger Delta, and educated at Government College, Ughelli, and University College, Ibadan. He has held fellowships at Princeton and Ibadan, and is now in the Department of English of the University of Lagos. Collections: *A Reed in the Tide, Casualties*; plays: *Song of a Goat, Ozidi*; also, *America Their America*, a critical look at the United States; poems in *Black Orpheus, Transition*, etc.

José Craveirinha   Born in 1922 in Lourenço Marques. Poet, journalist and outspoken critic of the colonial regime, he was arrested and tried with twelve other Mozambican intellectuals in 1966, and imprisoned as a FRELIMO supporter. Publication: *Chigubo*.

Viriato da Cruz   Born in 1928 in Porto Amboim, Angola. He was one of the initiators of the "Vamos descobrir Angola" movement, and editor of the radical literary magazine *Mensagem*. He was Secretary General of the People's Movement for the Liberation of Angola, MPLA, and is now a member of the Afro-Asian Writers Committee. Publications: *Poemas*, and numerous articles in *Revolution, Présence Africaine*, etc.

Bernard Dadié   Born in 1916 at Assinie, Ivory Coast, and educated in Dakar. For some years he worked in Dakar for the Institut Français d'Afrique Noire, and he is now in the government service in the Ivory Coast. Collections: *Afrique debout, La Ronde des Jours*; novels and collections of African legends and folk-tales: *Légendes africaines, Le pagne noir, Climbié, Un nègre à Paris. Hommes de tous les continents*.

Kaoberdiano Dambara   Born in 1939 in the Cape Verde Islands, and writes mainly in Guiné (Portuguese Guinea) Creole. He is a member of PAIGC, the Independence Party for Guiné and the Cabo Verdes.

Joe de Graft   A Ghanaian playwright, he initiated the Drama programme at the School of Music and Drama of the University of Ghana, and now works for UNESCO in Kenya. Publications: *Sons and Daughters* (play), *Visitor from the Past*.

Solomon Deressa   An Ethiopian who is fluent in Amharic, French and English. Collection: *The Tone of Silence*, a mid-century African portrait.

Noémia de Sousa   Born in 1927 in Lourenço Marques. She was very active politically during the 1950s when she was also producing her best poetry. She now lives quietly in Paris.

Birago Diop   Born in 1906 in Dakar. A veterinary surgeon by training, he has been Senegalese Ambassador to Tunisia and a member of the Senegalese cabinet. Collection: *Leurres et Lueurs*; folk-tales: *Les contes d'Amadou Koumba, Les nouveaux contes d'Amadou Koumba*; *Contes et lavanes*.

David Diop   Born in 1927 in Bordeaux of a Senegalese father and a Camerounian mother. He was a regular contributor to *Présence Africaine*, and published one collection, *Coups de pilon*, before he was killed in an air crash in 1960.

Mbella Sonne Dipoko   Born in 1936 in Douala, Cameroon, but grew up in Western Cameroon and Nigeria. He joined the Nigerian Broadcasting Corporation in 1958, but has lived in France since 1960 where he studied law for a time. Collection: *Black and White in Love*; play: *Overseas*; novels: *A Few Nights and Days, Because of Women*; numerous articles, short stories, poems.

Marcelino dos Santos   Born in 1929 in Mozambique. He studied political science at the Sorbonne and remained in France for ten years as a political exile. He returned to Africa when FRELIMO was formed and is a member of the Council of Presidency. His poems have been widely translated and collections have been published in Moscow.

Tsegaye Gabre-Medhin   Born in Ethiopia, where he is Director of the Haile Selassie I Theatre in Addis Ababa. He has published many plays in Amharic, including adaptations of *Othello* and *Macbeth*, and, in English, *Oda-Oak Oracle*. A collection of his poems appeared in the *Ethiopian Observer*.

Armando Guebuza   Born in 1942 in Mozambique, and educated in Lourenço Marques. He has been FRELIMO Inspector of Schools, in charge of the primary school programme.

Ismael Hurreh   Born in Hargeisa, Northern Region of Somalia. Educated at the University of New Mexico, he teaches in Mogadishu.

Antonio Jacinto   Born in 1932 in Luanda, Angola. A militant nationalist, he was condemned to fourteen years' imprisonment on political charges. Collection: *Poemas*.

Paulin Joachim   Born in Senegal. Formerly correspondent for the magazine *Bingo*, now director of *Décennie 2*. Publications: *Un nègre raconte*; poems in *Présence Africaine*.

Charles Kabuto Kabuye   Ugandan. Published in *Dhana*.

W. Kamera   Born in 1942 at Mwika Moshi, Kilimanjaro, and educated at Ilboru, Arusha, and at what was the University of East Africa at Dar es Salaam, and Cornell University. He is now a member of the Department of Literature at the University of Dar es Salaam. Published in *Transition*, *Zuka*.

Jonathan Kariara   An editor with Oxford University Press in Nairobi, he has published many short stories and poems, in particular in *Zuka*.

Amin Kassam   Born in 1948 in Mombasa, he was once assistant editor of *Busara*. Poems and short stories published in *Drum Beat*, *Busara*, etc, and broadcast over Radio Uganda, Voice of Kenya, and the BBC.

Yusuf O. Kassam   Born in 1943 in Tanzania, and educated at Makerere University in Uganda. He is now a member of the Institute of Adult Education at the University of Dar es Salaam. Published in *Young Commonwealth Poets '65*, *New Voices of the Commonwealth*, and numerous journals, and broadcast over the BBC African Service.

Keorapetse Kgositsile   Born in Johannesburg, and educated at Lincoln University, the University of New Hampshire, and the New School of Social Research in New York City. He is currently attached to the Columbia University Writing Program in New York. Collections: *Spirits Unchained*, *For Melba*; poems in anthologies, *Black Fire*, *Modern Poetry from Africa* and *Poems Now*, and in *Transition*, *Guerrilla*, etc.

Kittobbe   Ugandan. Published in *Dhana*.

Mazisi Kunene   Born in 1930 in Durban, and educated at Natal University. At present in England and actively engaged in political work. Author of a number of vernacular poems and plays some of which have been published in South Africa. Collection: *Zulu Poems*.

Kojo Gyinaye Kyei   Born in 1932 in Ghana, and educated in America. He is an architect by training, as well as being a poet and painter. Collection: *The Lone Voice*.

Taban Lo Liyong   Born in 1938 in Uganda, he was the first African to receive a Master of Fine Arts degree from the Writers Workshop of the University of Iowa. He is now a lecturer in English at the University of Nairobi. Publications: *Fixions* (stories), *Eating Chiefs* (personal transmutation of Lwo poetry), *The Last Word* (literary criticism), *Frantz Fanon's Uneven Ribs* (poems).

Stephen Lubega   Born in 1945 in Masaka District, Uganda, and educated at Bukalasa Seminary, the National Teachers' College, Kyambogo, and Makerere University. He has taught in secondary schools and was the first editor of *Student Lines*. Published in *Zuka*, *Flamingo*, and broadcast over the BBC African Service.

Theo Luzuka   Editor of *Dhana*, he is at the Department of English Language and Literature of the University of Singapore.

Valente Malangatana   Born in 1936 in Marracuene, Mozambique, he is a well-known painter as well as poet. He lives in Lourenço Marques where he spent some time in jail on political grounds. Published in *Black Orpheus*, etc, and *Modern Poetry from Africa*.

Ifeanyi Menkiti   Born in 1940 in Onitsha, Nigeria, and educated at Columbia University and Pomona College, California. Novel: *Affirmations*; poems published in *Evergreen Review*, *Liberator*, *African Arts*, *Transition*, etc.

Mindelense   Born in Portuguese Guinea, he works with the PAIGC.

Oswald Mbuyiseni Mtshali   Born in 1940, in South Africa, he lives in Johannesburg. Collection: *Sounds of a Cowhide Drum*.

Agostinho Neto   Born in 1922 in the Catete region of Angola, he studied medicine in Lisbon and Coimbra. A militant nationalist, he has served several terms of imprisonment. He is now President of MPLA. Collection: *A sagrada Esperança*; poems published in Portuguese and Angolan reviews and in anthology.

Arthur Nortje   Born in 1942 in Oudtshoorn in the Cape Province of South Africa, and educated in Port Elizabeth and at the segregated University College of the Western Cape and at Jesus College, Oxford. He taught in Canada before returning to Oxford where he died in 1970. Collection: *Dead Roots*; poems in anthologies, *Modern Poetry from Africa*, *Seven South African Poets*, and in *Black Orpheus*, *African Arts*, etc.

Richard Ntiru   Born in 1946 near Kisoro, Uganda, and educated at Ntare School, Nbarara, and Makerere University where he edited the campus newspaper and the campus journal of creative writing, and organised the 1969 Arts Festival. Collection: *Tensions*; also radio plays and short stories, and poems published in *Zuka*, etc.

Atukwei Okai   Born in 1941 in Accra, and educated at schools in Ghana before taking his MA(Litt) at the Gorky Literary Institute in Moscow, and his MPhil at the University of London. He is lecturer in

Russian at the Department of Modern Languages of the University of Ghana at Legon, and is President of the Ghana Association of Writers. Collections: *Flowerfall, The Oath of the Fontomfrom, Lorgorligi Logarithms, Rhododendrons in Donkeydom*; poems published in *Okyeame, Atlantic Monthly, New American Review*, etc.

Gabriel Okara   Born in 1921 in the Ijaw district of the Niger Delta, he trained as a book-binder, and worked in Enugu for the Information Service of Eastern Nigeria. Novel: *The Voice*; poems in *Modern Poetry from Africa* and *Black Orpheus*, etc.

Christopher Okigbo   Born in 1932 in Ojoto, Eastern Nigeria, and died on the Nsukka battlefront in 1967. He studied classics at the University College, Ibadan, and became Private Secretary to the Federal Minister of Research and Information before working as librarian at the University of Nigeria, and then as Manager in West Africa for the Cambridge University Press. Collections: *Heavensgate*, included in *Labyrinths, The Limits*; poems published in *Black Orpheus, Transition*, etc.

Yambo Ouologuem   Born in 1940 in Mali, and educated in Bamako and Paris. His novel *Le Devoir de Violence (Bound to Violence)* won the Prix Renaudot in 1968.

Frank Kobina Parkes   Born in 1932 at Korle Bu, Ghana. He has been a clerk, a reporter, an editor and a radio producer. Published in *Okyeame*, etc.

Okot p'Bitek   Born in 1931 in Gulu, Uganda, and educated at King's College, Budo, and at the Universities of Bristol, Aberystwyth and Oxford. He has lectured at Makerere and in the USA, and was Director of the National Theatre, Kampala. He now works in the Institute of African Studies at the University of Nairobi. Publications: *Two Songs*, and poems and articles in East African journals.

Lenrie Peters   Born in 1932 in Bathurst, Gambia, and educated at the Prince of Wales School, Freetown, and Trinity College, Cambridge. He trained and worked at various hospitals in Britain before returning to Gambia where he is a surgeon. Collections: *Satellites, Katchikali*.

Rabéarivelo   Born in 1901 at Antananarivo, Madagascar. He wrote poetry in both French and Spanish as well as in his native Malagasy. He founded a literary review and led the way in the creation of a new Madagascan literature written in French. He committed suicide in 1937. Collections: *La Coupe de Cendres, Sylves, Volumes, Vientes de la Manana, Presque Songes, Traduit de la Nuit, Vieilles Chansons du Pays d'Imerina*.

Isaac Rammopo   A member of the Advanced Teachers' College at Zaria, Nigeria.

Jorge Rebelo   Born in 1940 in Lourenço Marques and educated at ˜imbra University. He is FRELIMO Secretary for Information and edits the magazine *Mozambique Revolution*.

Arnaldo Santos   Born in 1936 in Luanda, Angola, he is a poet and short-story writer. Publications: *Fuga, Quinaxixe*.

L. S. Senghor   Born in 1906 in Joal, and educated at lycées in Dakar and Paris and at the Sorbonne. He taught in France until called up at the outbreak of war in Europe, and was for some time a prisoner-of-war in Germany. After liberation, he became a Deputy in the French Assemblée Nationale, and led the group of politicians who obtained independence for the French African colonies. He has been President of the Republic of Senegal since 1960. In 1948 he published the important *Anthologie de la nouvelle poésie nègre et malgache*. Collections: *Chants d'ombre, Hosties noires, Chants pour Naëtt, Ethiopiques, Nocturnes, Selected Poems*.

Onésimo Silveira   Born in 1936 in the Cape Verde Islands, he lived in San Tomé for three years and spent some time working as a civil servant in Angola. He joined PAIGC and acted as European representative while studying in Sweden. Collection: *Hora Grande*; essay: "Conscienscialização na Literatura de Cabo Verde".

Wole Soyinka   Born in 1934 in Nigeria, and educated at the Universities of Ibadan and Lagos. He has lectured at the Universities of Ife and Lagos, has been Head of the Department of Theatre Arts of the University of Ibadan, and was recently Visiting Fellow at Churchill College, Cambridge. Plays: *The Road, The Lion and the Jewel, Madmen and Specialists*, etc; collections: *Idanre, A Shuttle in the Crypt*; work also published in *Transition, Black Orpheus, New Statesman*, etc.

J.-B. Tati-Loutard   Born in 1938 at Pointe Noire, Congo (Brazzaville), and educated in Brazzaville and at the University of Bordeaux. He returned to Brazzaville in 1966 where he taught literature at the Centre d'Enseignement Supérieur and at the Ecole Normale Supérieure d'Afrique Centrale, and is now Dean of the Faculté des Lettres et Sciences Humaines of the University of Brazzaville. Collections: *Poèmes de la mer, Les racines congolaises*.

Bahadur Tejani   Born on the slopes of Kilimanjaro, and educated at the Universities of Makerere and Cambridge. He lectures at the University of Nairobi. Publications: *The Rape of Literature* (protest on India), *Day After Tomorrow* (novel), articles and poems.

B. S. Tibenderana   A student at Makerere University. Published in *Student Lines, Pulsations*.

Enoch Tindimwebwa   A student at Makerere University. Published in *Pulsations*, etc.

Kalu Uka   Born in Eastern Nigeria. He runs a theatre group at the University of Nigeria at Nsukka. Published in *Okike*, etc.

Tchicaya U Tam'si   Born in 1931 at Mpili, Congo (Brazzaville), and educated at lycées in Orleans and Paris. For a period during the crisis year of 1960 he was Chief Editor of the new daily, *Le Congo*. He now works for UNESCO in Paris. Collections: *Le mauvais sang, Feu de brousse, A triche-coeur, Epitomé, Le ventre, Arc musical*, and, in translation, *Brush Fire, Selected Poems*.

Okogbule Wonodi   Born in 1936 at Diobu near Port Harcourt, Eastern Nigeria, and educated at the University of Nigeria at Nsukka. Collection: *Icheke*; published in *Transition, Black Orpheus*, etc.

Note on Translations

AFRICAN WRITERS SERIES

Note on Translations

From the Bakiga

Okumu-Pa'lukobo translated "Eye of a calf . . ." and "Sorghum, sorghum, O sorghum . . .".

From the French

Ulli Beier translated "The black glassmaker . . .", "Pomegranate", "There you stand . . .", "Three Birds" and "Zebu" by Rabéarivelo.

Gerald Moore translated "Agony" and "Fragile" by Tchicaya U Tam'si.

Gerald Moore and Ulli Beier translated "Vanity" by Birago Diop, "Listen Comrades" by David Diop.

John Reed and Clive Wake translated "O tulip, tulip I have chosen . . ." by Siriman Cissoko, "I Thank You God" and "Leaf in the Wind" by Bernard Dadié, "Breath" by Birago Diop, "The Right Road" and "Sell Out" by David Diop, "Anti-Grace" by Paulin Joachim, "Tomatoes" by Yambo Ouologuem, "Cactus" and "Daybreak" by Rabéarivelo, "Elegy of the Circumcized", "Elegy of Midnight", "A hand of light caressed my eyelids . . .", "I came with you as far as the village of grain-huts . . .", 'I have spun a song soft as a murmur of doves . . .', "Is it surprising my dear . . .", "Letter to a Poet", "Long, long have you held between your hands . . .", "Murders" and "Was it a Mograbin night..." by L. S. Senghor, "Transformation Scenes" by J.-B. Tati-Loutard, "As best he can each dies alone . . .", "Communion", "Matting to Weave" and "Presence" by Tchicaya U Tam'si.

From the Portuguese

Margaret Dickinson translated "Fourth Poem" by Costa Andrade, "Mamana Saquina" and "Mamparra M'gaiza" by José Craveirinha, "Black Mother" by Viriato da Cruz, "Judgment of the Black Man" by Kaoberdiano Dambara, "If You Want to Know Me" and "The Poem of João" by Noémia de Sousa, "Here We Were Born" by Marcelino dos Santos, "Those Strange Times" by Armando Guebuza, "Love Poem" by Antonio Jacinto, "Attention" by Mindelense, "African Poetry", "February", "Hoisting the Flag" and "Western Civilization" by Agostinho Neto, "Poem" by Jorge Rebelo, "The Return" by Arnaldo Santos, "A Different Poem" and "The Long Day's March" by Onésimo Silveira.

Dorothy Guedes and Philippa Rumsey translated "Woman" by Valente Malangatana.

From the Swahili

Lyndon Harries translated "Give me the minstrel's seat . . .", "O apster of soured wine . . .", "Praise my bow with haft of the wild-vine", "Serenade".

From the Yoruba

Babalola translated "At a Thrift-Club Feast" and "Now I will chant a salute to my Ogun . . .".

Bakare Gbadamosi and Ulli Beier translated "The hunter dies . . ." and "Slowly the muddy pool becomes a river . . .".

Miriam Koshland translated "Cuckold Contented" from the French version adapted by Leon Dumas.

Ademola Oniton-Okuta and Ulli Beier translated "Incantation to Cause the Rebirth of a Dead Child" and "Incantation to Bring Popularity".

From the Fulani

Malam Hampate Ba translated "The Fulani Creation Story".

From the Zulu

Trevor Cope translated "Ndela, Son of Sompisi".

Acknowledgments

Acknowledgments

The editor and his publishers gratefully acknowledge the permission of the poets and their respective publishers to reprint the poems in this anthology.

Abangira: "Stance—a Tribute" first appeared in *Dhana* (East African Literature Bureau).

G. Adali-Mortty: "Belonging" from *Messages: Poems from Ghana* edited by Kofi Awoonor and G. Adali-Mortty (Heinemann Educational Books Ltd).

Costa Andrade: "Fourth Poem" from *When Bullets Begin to Flower* selected and translated by Margaret Dickinson (East African Publishing House).

Jared Angira: "Masked" from *Juices* by Jared Angira (East African Publishing House). "Phlora" from *Pulsations* (East African Literature Bureau). "Expelled", "Femi-Aura", "Hitch-Hike", "If", "A Look in the Past", "My Mother Who Art . . .", "No Coffin, No Grave", "Rosbella Adhiambo", "She Has Not Dreamt", "The Sprinter", "Were I Clever" from *Silent Voices* by Jared Angira (Heinemann Educational Books Ltd)

Peter Anyang'-Nyong'O: "Daughter of the Low Land" from *Poems from East Africa* edited by David Cook and David Rubadiri (Heinemann Educational Books Ltd).

Kofi Awoonor: "The Journey Beyond" from *Messages: Poems from Ghana* edited by Kofi Awoonor and G. Adali-Mortty (Heinemann Educational Books Ltd). "Songs of Sorrow" from *Night of My Blood* by Kofi Awoonor, copyright © 1971 by Kofi Awoonor. Used by permission of Doubleday & Company, Inc.

Kwesi Brew: "Ancestral Faces" from *A Book of African Verse* edited by John Reed and Clive Wake (Heinemann Educational Books Ltd). "The Harvest of Our Life" from *Shadows of Laughter* by Kwesi Brew (Longman Group Ltd and Longman, Inc). "The Mesh" from *West African Verse* edited by D. T. Nwoga (Longman Group Ltd and Humanities Press, Inc).

Dennis Brutus: all poems from *A Simple Lust* by Dennis Brutus, copyright © Dennis Brutus 1963, 1968, 1970, 1971 and 1973 (Heinemann Educational Books Ltd and Hill & Wang).

Siriman Cissoko: "O tulip, tulip I have chosen . . ." from *French African Verse* selected and translated by John Reed and Clive Wake (Heinemann Educational Books Ltd). Originally in French in *Ressac de nous-mémes* (Présence Africaine).

J. P. Clark: "Agbor Dancer", "His Excellency the Masquerader" from *A Reed in the Tide* by J. P. Clark (Longman Group Ltd and Longman, Inc.) "The Casualties" from *Casualties* by J. P. Clark (Longman Group

Ltd and Longman, Inc). "Ibadan" from *A Book of African Verse* edited by John Reed and Clive Wake (Heinemann Educational Books Ltd).

José Craveirinha: "Mamana Saquina", "Mamparra M'gaiza" from *When Bullets Begin to Flower* selected and translated by Margaret Dickinson (East African Publishing House).

Viriato da Cruz: "Black Mother" from *When Bullets Begin to Flower* selected and translated by Margaret Dickinson (East African Publishing House).

Bernard Dadié: "I Thank You God", "Leaf in the Wind" from *French African Verse* selected and translated by John Reed and Clive Wake (Heinemann Educational Books Ltd). Originally in French in *La ronde des jours* (Seghers).

Kaoberdiano Dambara: "Judgment of the Black Man" from *When Bullets Begin to Flower* selected and translated by Margaret Dickinson (East African Publishing House).

Keki Darwulla: "Black Rain" first appeared in *Black Orpheus 22*.

Joe de Graft: "Akosua 'Nowa" from *Messages: Poems from Ghana* edited by Kofi Awoonor and G. Adali-Mortty (Heinemann Educational Books Ltd).

Solomon Deressa: "Shifting Gears" first appeared in *African Arts*, Spring 1969.

Noémia de Sousa: "If You Want to Know Me", "The Poem of João" from *When Bullets Begin to Flower* selected and translated by Margaret Dickinson (East African Publishing House).

Birago Diop: "Breath" from *French African Verse* selected and translated by John Reed and Clive Wake (Heinemann Educational Books Ltd). "Vanity" from *Modern Poetry from Africa* edited by Gerald Moore and Ulli Beier, translation copyright © Gerald Moore and Ulli Beier, 1963 (Penguin African Library). Both originally in French in *Leurres et lueurs* (Présence Africaine).

David Diop: "Listen Comrades" from *Modern Poetry from Africa* edited by Gerald Moore and Ulli Beier, translation copyright © Gerald Moore and Ulli Beier, 1963 (Penguin African Library). "The Right Road", "Sell-Out" from *French African Verse* selected and translated by John Reed and Clive Wake (Heinemann Educational Books Ltd). All originally in French in *Coups de pilon* (Présence Africaine).

Mbella Sonne Dipoko: "Compassion", "Heroic Shields", "Rulers", "Upheaval" first appeared in *Black Orpheus 20*.

Marcelino dos Santos: "Here We Were Born" from *When Bullets Begin to Flower* selected and translated by Margaret Dickinson (East African Publishing House).

Armando Guebuza: "Those Strange Times" from *When Bullets Begin to Flower* selected and translated by Margaret Dickinson (East African Publishing House).

Ismael Hurreh: "Abidjan", "Foreboding", "Pardon Me" first appeared **in** *Transition* 28.

Antonio Jacinto: "Love Poem" from *When Bullets Begin to Flower* **selected** and translated by Margaret Dickinson (East African Publish-**ing House**).

Paulin Joachim: "Anti-Grace" from *French African Verse* selected and **translated** by John Reed and Clive Wake (Heinemann Educational **Books** Ltd). Originally in French in *Anti-grâce* (Présence Africaine).

Charles Kabuto Kabuye: "The Great Escapes", "The Struggle" first **appeared** in *Dhana* (East African Literature Bureau).

W. Kamera: "Poem in Four Parts" from *Poems from East Africa* edited by **David** Cook and David Rubadiri (Heinemann Educational Books Ltd).

Jonathan Kariara: "Grass Will Grow" first appeared in *Zuka* (Oxford University Press, East Africa).

Amin Kassam: "The Desert", "Fashion", "Metamorphosis", "Trapped **in a Puddle**" from *Pulsations* (East African Literature Bureau). "Martin **Luther** King" from *Poems from East Africa* edited by David Cook and **David** Rubadiri (Heinemann Educational Books Ltd).

Yussuf O. Kassam: "Maji Maji" from *Poems of East Africa* edited by **David** Cook and David Rubadiri (Heinemann Educational Books **Ltd**).

Keorapetse Kgositsile: "Mandela's Sermon" from *Spirits Unchained* **(Broadside** Press). "Notes from No Sanctuary", "Point of Departure" **from** *My Name is Afrika* by Keorapetse Kgositsile, copyright © 1971 by **Keorapetse** Kgositsile. Used by permission of Doubleday & Company, **Inc.**

Kittobbe: "To the Childless" first appeared in *Dhana* (East African **Literature** Bureau).

Mazisi Kunene: "The Echoes" from *Modern Poetry from Africa*, edited by **Gerald** Moore and Ulli Beier (Penguin African Library). All other **poems** reprinted from *Zulu Poems* by Mazisi Kunene, copyright © **Mazisi** Kunene 1970, by permission of André Deutsch Ltd, London, **and** Africana Publishing Company, New York.

Kojo Gyinaye Kyei: "Time" from *Messages: Poems from Ghana* edited by **Kofi** Awoonor and G. Adali-Mortty (Heinemann Educational Books **Ltd**).

Taban Lo Liyong: "To Susan Sontag, with love" from *Frantz Fanon's Uneven Ribs* by Taban Lo Liyong (Heinemann Educational Books Ltd).

Stephen Lubega: "Evening" first appeared in *Zuka* (Oxford University **Press**, East Africa).

Theo Luzuka: "The Motoka" first appeared in *Dhana* (East African **Literature** Bureau).

Susan Lwanga: "Daybreak" from *Pulsations* (East African Literature **Bureau**).

Valente Malangatana: "Woman" translation reprinted by permission of Philippa Rumsey.

Sam Mbure: "To a Bed-Bug" from *Pulsations* (East African Literature Bureau).

Ifeanyi Menkiti: "Heart of the Matter" reprinted by permission of The Third Press.

Mindelense: "Attention" from *When Bullets Begin to Flower* selected and translated by Margaret Dickinson (East African Publishing House).

Oswald Mbuyiseni Mtshali: all poems from *Sounds of a Cowhide Drum* by Oswald Mbuyiseni Mtshali, copyright © Oswald Mbuyiseni Mtshali 1971. Reprinted by permission of Oxford University Press, London, and Oxford University Press, Inc, New York.

Agostinho Neto: "African Poetry", "February", "Hoisting the Flag", "Western Civilization" from *When Bullets Begin to Flower* selected and translated by Margaret Dickinson (East African Publishing House).

Arthur Nortje: all poems from *Dead Roots* by Arthur Nortje (Heinemann Educational Books Ltd).

Richard Ntiru: "The Pauper", "To the Living" from *Poems from East Africa* edited by David Cook and David Rubadiri (Heinemann Educational Books Ltd).

Gabriel Okara: "You Laughed and Laughed and Laughed" from *Commonwealth Poets of Today* edited by Howard Sergeant (John Murray Ltd for The English Association).

Christopher Okigbo: "Heavensgate" reprinted from *Labyrinths with Path of Thunder* by Christopher Okigbo, © 1971 Legal Personal Representatives of Christopher Okigbo, by permission of Heinemann Educational Books Ltd, London, and Africana Publishing Company, New York.

Yambo Ouologuem: "Tomatoes" from *French African Verse* selected and translated by John Reed and Clive Wake (Heinemann Educational Books Ltd). Originally in French in *Nouvelle somme de la posée de la monde noire* (Présence Africaine).

Frank Kobina Parkes: "Redemption" from *Messages: Poems from Ghana* edited by Kofi Awoonor and G. Adali-Mortty (Heinemann Educational Books Ltd).

Okot p'Bitek: "Song of Malaya" from *Two Songs* by Okot p'Bitek (East African Publishing House).

Lenrie Peters: "Autumn burns me . . .", "Lost Friends", "Mine is the silent face . . .", "On a wet September morning . . .", "The panic of growing older . . .", "Parachute men say . . .", "Turning the pages of my diary slowly . . .", "Watching someone die" . . . from *Satellites* by Lenrie Peters (Heinemann Educational Books Ltd). "He walks alone . . .", "Isatou died . . .", "It is time for reckoning Africa . . .", "I are is juxtaposed to the Ego . . .", "The sun has paled and turned away . . .", "You lie there naked . . ." from *Katchikali* by Lenrie Peters (Heinemann Educational Books Ltd).

Rabéarivelo: "Cactus", "Daybreak" from *A Book of African Verse* edited by John Reed and Clive Wake (Heinemann Educational Books Ltd).

Isaac Rammopo: "A Moment Already Gone", "Requiem for the Saboteurs" first appeared in *Black Orpheus 20*.

Jorge Rebelo: "Poem" from *When Bullets Begin to Flower* selected and translated by Margaret Dickinson (East African Publishing House).

Roderic R. Roberts: "On Friendship and War" from *Pulsations* (East African Literature Bureau).

Arnaldo Santos: "The Return" from *When Bullets Begin to Flower* selected and translated by Margaret Dickinson (East African Publishing House).

L. S. Senghor: "Elegy of the Circumcized", "Elegy of Midnight", "Is it surprising my dear . . .", "Long, long have you held between your hands . . ." from *Selected Poems* by Léopold Sédar Senghor translated by John Reed and Clive Wake, © Oxford University Press 1964. Reprinted by permission of Oxford University Press and Atheneum Publishers. "A hand of light caressed my eyelids . . .", "I came with you as far as the village of grain huts . . .", "I have spun a song soft as a murmur of doves . . .", "Was it a Mograbin night . . ." from *Nocturnes* by L. S. Senghor translated by John Reed and Clive Wake, © Editions du Seuil 1961, translation copyright © John P .d and Clive Wake 1969. Reprinted by permission of Heinemann ducational Books ʰ and The Third Press. "Letter to a Poet", "Murders" from *French African Verse* selected and translated by John Reed and Clive Wake (Heinemann Educational Books Ltd).

Onésimo Silveira: "A Different Poem", "The Long Day's March" from *When Bullets Begin to Flower* selected and translated by Margaret Dickinson (East African Publishing House).

Tom Simpson: "African Communion", "Freight Train" from *Pulsations* (East African Literature Bureau).

Wole Soyinka: "IV The Beginning", "Dedication", "Fado Singer", "Post Mortem", "To My First White Hairs" from *Idanre and Other Poems* by Wole Soyinka, © Wole Soyinka 1967 (Methuen & Company Ltd and Hill & Wang). "Capital", "Gulliver", "Purgatory", "Ulysses" from *A Shuttle in the Crypt* by Wole Soyinka, © Wole Soyinka 1972 (Rex Collins Ltd with Eyre Methuen Ltd and Hill & Wang).

.-B. Tati-Loutard: "Transformation Scenes" from *French African Verse* selected and translated by John Reed and Clive Wake (Heinemann Educational Books Ltd). Originally in French in *Poèmes de la mer* (Editions CLE, Yaoundé).

Bahadur Tejani: "The Analogy", "Leaving the Country", "Lines for a Hindi Poet" from *Pulsations* (East African Literature Bureau).

B. S. Tibenderana: "The Bastard" from *Pulsations* (East African Literature Bureau).

Enoch Tindimwebwa: "The White Pumpkin" from *Pulsations* (East African Literature Bureau).

Traditional: "Love Song", "The Fulani Creation Story", "Incantation to Cause the Rebirth of a Dead Child", "Incantation to Gain Popularity" first appeared in *Black Orpheus 19*, "Cuckold Contented" in *Black Orpheus 6*, "The hunter dies . . .", "Slowly the muddy pool becomes a river . . ." in *Black Orpheus 22*. "Eye of a calf . . .", "Sorghum, sorghum, O sorghum . . ." from *Pulsations* (East African Literature Bureau). "Give me the minstrel's seat . . .", "O tapster of soured wine . . .", "Praise my bow with haft of the wild-vine . . .", "Serenade" from *Swahili Poetry* edited by Lyndon Harries, © 1962 Oxford University Press, by permission of The Clarendon Press, Oxford, and Oxford University Press, Inc, New York. "At a Thrift-Club Feast", "Now I will chant a salute to my Ogun . . ." from *The Content and Form of Yoruba Ijala* by Babalola, © 1966 Oxford University Press, by permission of The Clarendon Press, Oxford, and Oxford University Press, Inc, New York. "Ndela, Son of Sompisi" from *Izibongo Zulu Praise-Poems* edited by Trevor Cope, © 1968 Oxford University Press, by permission of The Clarendon Press, Oxford, and Oxford University Press, Inc, New York. "To Palm Wine" from *Reflections: Nigerian Prose and Verse* (African Universities Press).

Kalu Uka: "New Order" first appeared in *Okike* No. 1 (University of Nigeria, Nsukka). **Tchicaya U Tam'si**: "Agony", "Fragile" from *Selected Poems* by Tchicaya U Tam'si translated by Gerald Moore (Heinemann Educational Books Ltd). "As best he can each dies alone . . .", "Communion", "Matting to Weave", "Presence" from *French African Verse* selected and translated by John Reed and Clive Wake (Heinemann Educational Books Ltd). Originally in French in, respectively, *A triche-coeur* (P.-J. Oswald, Paris), *Epitomé* (P.-J. Oswald, Tunis), *Le ventre* (Présence Africaine), *Arc musical* (P.-J. Oswald, Honfluer), *Feu de brousse* (Caractères) and *Feu de brousse*.

Okogbule Wonodi: "On the Edge" first appeared in *Black Orpheus 19*.

THE AFRICAN AND CARIBBEAN WRITERS SERIES

The book you have been reading is part of the *Heinemann African Poets* Series. Details of some of the other titles available are given below, but for a catalogue giving information on the whole series and the long established *African and Caribbean Writers Series* write to:
Heinemann International Literature and Textbooks
Halley Court, Jordan Hill, Oxford OX2 8EJ

KOFI ANYIDOHO, PETER PORTER AND MUSAEMURA ZIMUNYA (ED'S)
The Fate of Vultures

This innovative selection of African poems from some 4500 entries submitted for the 1988 BBC Arts and Africa Poetry Award, reflects the great depth and vigour of contemporary African Poetry.

SYL CHENEY-COKER
The Blood in The Desert's Eye

'Cheney-Coker strikes me as one of the very few poets in Africa who belong to the international community of letters. Not only does he stand head and shoulders above the others but he refuses to be confined within the denomination "African poet", aiming at something closer to universality . . . Among the most energetic poets writing in Africa.'
Robert Fraser

FRANK CHIPASULA
Whispers in the Wings

'(Frank Chipasula) offers some of the most vivid imagery in
all modern African verse.'
*Adrian Roscoe, The Quiet Chameleon: Modern Poetry from
Central Africa*

KOJO LAING
Godhorse

This is a powerful, witty and original collection by Ghana's
leading novelist and poet.
Laing's intense yet often playful treatment of themes such as
nature, love, death, politics and portraits of daily life ensures that
Godhorse makes for evocative, ironic and humorous reading.

ADEWALE MAJA-PEARCE (ED)
The Heinemann Book of African
Poetry in English

This anthology represents the best African Poetry written in
English over the last thirty years. It includes the work of
familiar names such as Wole Soyinka, Dennis Brutus and
Kojo Laing as well as new talent from the younger generation
which includes Chenjerai Hove and Gabriel Gbadamosi.